Books Published by AA Grapevine, Inc.

The Language of the Heart (& eBook)

The Best of the Grapevine Volumes I, II, III

The Best of Bill (& eBook)

Thank You for Sharing

Spiritual Awakenings I & II (& eBooks)

I Am Responsible: The Hand of AA

Emotional Sobriety I & II—The Next Frontier (& eBooks)

In Our Own Words: Stories of Young AAs in Recovery (& eBook)

Beginners' Book (& eBook)

Voices of Long-Term Sobriety (& eBook)

A Rabbit Walks Into A Bar

Step by Step—Real AAs, Real Recovery (& eBook)

Young & Sober (& eBook)

Into Action (& eBook)

Happy, Joyous & Free (& eBook)

One on One (& eBook)

No Matter What (& eBook)

Grapevine Daily Quote Book (& eBook)

Sober & Out (& eBook)

Forming True Partnerships (& eBook)

Our Twelve Traditions (& eBook)

Making Amends (& eBook)

Voices of Women in AA (& eBook)

AA in the Military (& eBook)

One Big Tent (& eBook)

Take Me to Your Sponsor (& eBook)

Free on the Inside (& eBook)

Prayer & Meditation (& eBook)

Fun in Sobriety (& eBook)

The Home Group: Heartbeat of AA-30th Anniversary Ed. (& eBook)

Our Twelve Steps (& eBook)

IN SPANISH

El lenguaje del corazón

Lo mejor de Bill (& eBook)

El grupo base: Corazón de AA

Lo mejor de La Viña

Felices, alegres y libres (& eBook)

Un día a la vez (& eBook)

Frente A Frente (& eBook)

Bajo El Mismo Techo (& eBook)

Sobriedad emocional (& eBook)

IN FRENCH

Le langage du coeur

Les meilleurs articles de Bill

Le Groupe d'attache: Le battement du coeur des AA

En tête à tête (& eBook)

Heureux, joyeux et libres (& eBook)

La sobriété émotive

Collector's Edition

The Next Frontier

Emotional Sobriety I & II

AA Grapevine

475 Riverside Drive, New York, New York 10115

ISBN: 978-1-938642-94-4

Second Printing 2026

AA Preamble

Alcoholics Anonymous is a fellowship of people
who share their experience, strength and hope
with each other that they may solve their common problem
and help others to recover from alcoholism.

The only requirement for membership is a desire to stop drinking.
There are no dues or fees for AA membership;
we are self-supporting through our own contributions.
AA is not allied with any sect, denomination, politics,
organization or institution; does not wish to engage in any
controversy, neither endorses nor opposes any causes.

Our primary purpose is to stay sober
and help other alcoholics to achieve sobriety.

Contents

VOLUME II

PREFACE

This special collector's edition contains stories written by AA members that beautifully illustrate how much our lives can change for the better once we put the bottle down and come into Alcoholics Anonymous. In the January 1958 Grapevine our cofounder Bill W. wrote an essay called "The Next Frontier: Emotional Sobriety." It would become one of his most treasured writings. In 2006, AA Grapevine published the book *Emotional Sobriety, The Next Frontier* and followed it in 2011 with *Emotional Sobriety II.* They since have become two of our most beloved books, selling tens of thousands of copies each year. Both volumes are now bound together here for the first time. The stories inside show the many ways members have gained emotional sobriety as they work the program, incorporate the Twelve Steps into their lives, get involved in service and learn to help others. We hope you enjoy and share these powerful stories for years to come.

The Next Frontier—Emotional Sobriety

January 1958

I think that many oldsters who have put our AA "booze cure" to severe but successful tests still find they often lack emotional sobriety. Perhaps they will be the spearhead for the next major development in AA—the development of much more real maturity and balance (which is to say, humility) in our relations with ourselves, with our fellows, and with God.

Those adolescent urges that so many of us have for top approval, perfect security, and perfect romance—urges quite appropriate to age seventeen—prove to be an impossible way of life when we are at age forty-seven or fifty-seven.

Since AA began, I've taken immense wallops in all these areas because of my failure to grow up, emotionally and spiritually. My God, how painful it is to keep demanding the impossible, and how very painful to discover finally, that all along we have had the cart before the horse! Then comes the final agony of seeing how awfully wrong we have been, but still finding ourselves unable to get off the emotional merry-go-round.

How to translate a right mental conviction into a right emotional result, and so into easy, happy and good living—well, that's not only the neurotic's problem, it's the problem of life itself for all of us who have got to the point of real willingness to hew to right principles in all our affairs.

Even then, as we hew away, peace and joy may still elude us. That's the place so many of us AA oldsters have come to. And it's a hell of a spot, literally. How shall our unconscious—from which so many of our fears, compulsions and phony aspirations still stream—be brought into line with what we actually believe, know and want! How to convince our dumb, raging and hidden "Mr. Hyde" becomes our main task.

I've recently come to believe that this can be achieved. I believe so because I begin to see many benighted ones—folks like you and me—commencing to get results. Last autumn [several years back—ed.], depression, having no really rational cause at all, almost took me to the cleaners. I began to be scared that I was in for another long chronic spell. Considering the grief I've had with depressions, it wasn't a bright prospect.

I kept asking myself, "Why can't the Twelve Steps work to release depression?" By the hour, I stared at the St. Francis Prayer ... "It's better to comfort than to be comforted." Here was the formula, all right. But why didn't it work?

Suddenly I realized what the matter was. My basic flaw had always been dependence—almost absolute dependence—on people or circumstances to supply me with prestige, security, and the like. Failing to get these things according to my perfectionist dreams and specifications, I had fought for them. And when defeat came, so did my depression.

There wasn't a chance of making the outgoing love of St. Francis a workable and joyous way of life until these fatal and almost absolute dependencies were cut away.

Because I had over the years undergone a little spiritual development, the absolute quality of these frightful dependencies had never before been so starkly revealed. Reinforced by what Grace I could secure in prayer, I found I had to exert every ounce of will and action to cut off these faulty emotional dependencies upon people, upon AA, indeed, upon any set of circumstances whatsoever.

Then only could I be free to love as Francis had. Emotional and instinctual satisfactions, I saw, were really the extra dividends of having love, offering love, and expressing, a love appropriate to each relation of life.

Plainly, I could not avail myself of God's love until I was able to offer it back to Him by loving others as He would have me. And I couldn't possibly do that so long as I was victimized by false dependencies.

For my dependency meant demand—a demand for the possession and control of the people and the conditions surrounding me.

While those words "absolute dependency" may look like a gimmick, they were the ones that helped to trigger my release into my present degree of stability and quietness of mind, qualities which I am now trying to consolidate by offering love to others regardless of the return to me.

This seems to be the primary healing circuit: an outgoing love of God's creation and His people, by means of which we avail ourselves of His love for us. It is most clear that the real current can't flow until our paralyzing dependencies are broken, and broken at depth. Only then can we possibly have a glimmer of what adult love really is.

Spiritual calculus, you say? Not a bit of it. Watch any AA of six months working with a new Twelfth Step case. If the case says "To the devil with you" the Twelfth Stepper only smiles and turns to another case. He doesn't feel frustrated or rejected. If his next case responds, and in turn starts to give love and attention to other alcoholics, yet gives none back to him, the sponsor is happy about it anyway. He still doesn't feel rejected; instead he rejoices that his one-time prospect is sober and happy. And if his next following case turns out in later time to be his best friend (or romance) then the sponsor is most joyful. But he well knows that his happiness is a by-product—the extra dividend of giving without any demand for a return.

The really stabilizing thing for him was having and offering love to that strange drunk on his doorstep. That was Francis at work, powerful and practical, minus dependency and minus demand.

In the first six months of my own sobriety, I worked hard with many alcoholics. Not a one responded. Yet this work kept me sober. It wasn't a question of those alcoholics giving me anything. My stability came out of trying to give, not out of demanding that I receive.

Thus I think it can work out with emotional sobriety. If we examine every disturbance we have, great or small, we will find at the root of it some unhealthy dependency and its consequent unhealthy demand. Let us, with God's help, continually surrender these hobbling demands. Then we can be set free to live and love; we may then be able to Twelfth Step ourselves and others into emotional sobriety.

Of course I haven't offered you a really new idea—only a gimmick that has started to unhook several of my own "hexes" at depth. Nowadays my brain no longer races compulsively in either elation, grandiosity or depression. I have been given a quiet place in bright sunshine.

Bill W.

Volume I

Preface to Volume I

In 1958, the grapevine published an article by AA co-founder Bill W. about the ongoing challenges of recovery that he faced long after he stopped drinking. Called "The Next Frontier: Emotional Sobriety," the article describes Bill's insight that his struggle with depression was due to overweening dependencies on other people and outside circumstances. Bill explains how he had found peace of mind by letting go of his expectations and practicing what he calls "outgoing love" — a love less concerned with what one gets and more with what one gives. It was, as he put it, the St. Francis Prayer in action.

For some, the next frontier in recovery from alcoholism may be letting go of faulty, unrealistic dependencies; for others, it may mean illuminating persistent character defects or the "Now what?" malaise that can afflict the longtimer. The stories in this book show that when we have the willingness to find solutions rather than stay stuck in problems, we can let go of fear, selfishness, and resentment, put aside selfish demands, practice outgoing love, and become more connected to our Higher Power and our friends, family, and fellows.

This book does not represent a final definition of emotional sobriety. Growing up in sobriety means different things to each of us, and one's own idea of it may change over time. But one thing seems true: the rewards for reaching for emotional sobriety are serenity, emotional balance, and an increased joy in living.

— The Editors

SECTION 1

A New Perspective

"Some of us have tried to hold on to our old ideas and the result was nil until we let go absolutely."

– Alcoholics Anonymous, p.58

Old-timers sometimes say, "Staying sober is simple: Don't drink and change your whole life." The willingness to let go of old ways of thinking and behaving seems to be what emotional sobriety is all about. Once sober, we begin to let go of resentments and fears, self-pity and anger. We try to replace regrets about the past and worries about the future with faith in AA and AA's Twelve Steps and a power greater than ourselves. We used to see problems as insurmountable; now we take responsibility for finding solutions. And we find that, slowly, we can claim moments of real peace — "a quiet place in bright sunshine," as Bill W. puts it in the essay that gave the impetus to this book. For alcoholics, this is a true spiritual awakening.

Growth

June 1976

A new thought has been forming in my mind (now that the AA program has put it in working order). I believe that an element most important in building our sober lives is what is left out.

Several months ago, my husband and I enrolled in a beginners' art course. We didn't become great painters, but both of us now see things, such as leaves and blades of grass and shadings of color, that we weren't aware of before. One day, the instructor showed us a Picasso drawing of the artist's daughter. It pictured her in profile, and it consisted of only three lines. What was left out dramatized what was there. We learned also that in shading a tree, what is left out is as important as the pencil lines, for the blanks create sunlight on the leaves.

It seems to me that I achieve growth by leaving things out — when I don't say the cross word, when I don't answer sarcastically. If I can delay only one second, maybe two, I have time to ask myself, "Do I really want to say that?"

When I wrote down my list of people to make amends to, it was made up mostly of family. I wasn't just thinking of the things I had done. I also remembered the many things I should have, would have, might have done had I not been drinking! The things I had left out ranged from the nice bouquets I could have given, and didn't, all the way to downright neglect.

I used to tell all! To anybody who would listen! And things were going to be my way, too. "Self-will run riot!" Now it's becoming easier to spot ego, and I work at getting the big Me out of the way.

I have discovered a new way to learn — by shutting my mouth and listening. Again, it's not so much what I'm doing as what I'm not doing. I'm not talking. So I'm open; I'm teachable.

I used to like to direct my children's affairs, offering advice when it wasn't wanted and commanding activities and behavior. I'm more secure now. I've thrown out my director's chair. Now, when I see one of my children heading on a certain course and I question the outcome, I keep my mouth shut and practice the Third Step. Whenever there's a problem and I'm involved, I look to see what part of the problem I am causing (as one of my sponsors advised). I'm usually about eighty percent of the problem — well, maybe sixty percent, but the major part, you can bet on that. If I leave out the largest percent (me), there is hardly any problem at all!

I'm becoming so secure in AA, I've even discarded the cute, funny, phony me my civilian friends used to know. I don't have to dance with a rose in my teeth; I can just dance. And I don't have to be the only girl at the picnic who can swing Tarzan-style from a rope into the river. I can swim calmly, like the forty-year-old mother of four I am.

I don't have to show off long legs in a miniskirt any more. I can just sit on them and be happy. And I can say no to a lot of things I'm not interested in. All the people-pleasing activities I used to engage in, I can cut out now. That gives me time to do the truly helpful, gut-warming little things, just because they need doing and I truly care. I have time to work my program.

I can sit quietly and really listen to people trying to communicate with me. My mind is no longer racing to find just the perfect quip to say or story to top theirs.

The eternal internal war I can do without, too. The fighting inside me is over, and am I glad!

And the most important item of all to leave out is the old, familiar foe, alcohol. Without it, life is just plain wonderful!

Tricia J.
Houston, Texas

In All Our Affairs

July 1956

Words have a way of taking on an entirely new significance when we enter into the new world opened up to us by AA sobriety. We all know how the first apparent clichés of our simple formulas change and become a vital part of our daily life. We discover after a time, for example, that we never really had an inkling of how practically useful "think" is until we accept how very long it has been since we really understood it."Humility" came, with a bit more sobriety, to take its place as a lovely, living word, a quality of acceptance of our limitations, most devoutly to be searched for; the most desirable member of our family of words — humility.

"Gratitude," that much abused sister, also altered her face and was transformed into a joyful appreciation of our miraculous recovery. We grew to know that without daily gratitude our personal miracle would lose its lustre, and in time it could cover our shiny new world with a-dull-for-granted-taking that would lead us inevitably away from the fellowship and equally inevitably to our most welcoming enemy. We might drink if we became careless with our "gratitude."

"Pride" by a peculiar shift in syntax became the most active and omnipotent devil of a word, perhaps the most dangerous of all, and yet, while unresolved pride can lead us quickly to the bottle, we are tremendously proud that we are a part of AA.

"Honesty — " I heard an AA friend say at a meeting that he had heard a dictionary definition of honesty given by a rural postman at a country meeting in the middle-west. This old boy was sick of hearing this sensible word kicked around so he had gone to the County Court House and looked it up in "that big old dictionary there." It was good enough for him, it's good in any man's life. "Honesty — is the absence of the intent to deceive." Only what does "intent" mean?

Now I find that with all my new-found confidence in the validity and importance of semantics, I have been retarded and stifled by periodic waves of doubt and despair because of my blindness concerning the meaning of the key word to our entire program.

It occurs with perfect rightness in the Twelfth Step:"awakening."

Some hidden closet in my mind had failed to open. To me spiritual awakening meant an absolute conviction of and close relationship to a God everyone seemed to understand but me. I felt, in this untidy recess of my brain, that, without this revelation of spiritual grace, I couldn't begin to "carry the message" adequately and, of even greater importance, I was continually unsuccessful in handling "all my affairs."

I finally looked up the definition of awakening. It means to quicken, to stir, to wake up. It doesn't say anything about a great white light or an aura of divinity, in my dictionary.

Well, now I know without any more fuss or feathers, that I, like every other member of AA, have had a very tangible spiritual awakening. My belief in a Higher Power is as strong as it was when I went to my first AA meeting and accepted the first and second steps as simply and trustfully as a child accepts its mother's milk. And certainly AA with its never ending procession of miracles, has deepened and made tangible the evidence of the workings of that Higher Power. So what on earth was I looking for? I just don't know. I guess I wanted a little Tinker Bell all my own to show me the right and only way out of every situation.

In my peculiarly alcoholic way of creating difficulties, I discovered this semantic truth in the most involved way. Recently I was confronted with a work project that should have presented no particular difficulties, and yet it did. I blocked and blocked and couldn't rationally get around why I was procrastinating, fearful, unable to come to grips with it. I was thinking resentfully that in this year and a half in AA the only departments of my life that had become remotely manageable were my AA activities. I had no feelings of guilty inadequacy after I had been secretary of my group. I met my Grapevine deadlines. I spoke frequently at open and closed meetings. I had done everything requested or required of me without any anxiety as to the perfection of my performances.

Why was I having so much difficulty in the other areas of my life?

Quite suddenly and without any warning bells, the simple solution came to me. I had surrendered to only one thing: my alcoholism. I accepted divine and temporal help in everything that had to do with my disease with complete humility but I never had extended this wonderful freedom from pride, resentments, envy and need for perfection and competition into "all my affairs."

So it finally came to me in this time of really deep need: I had had no understanding of the meaning of spiritual awakening. And because I accepted all things in AA as natural and just and healthy and good, I was only permitting an unconscious use of my spiritual awakening in AA areas. And I had never brought it out and looked at it before.

Now I hope and pray I can indeed carry to all my affairs the conscious use of surrender and humility and gratitude, employing them with the knowledge that, if I do, my affairs, under God's direction have a better chance of reaching a daily truth.

H.W.
Westport, Connecticut

Win Or Lose

August 2001

As a hard-charging marketer, I used to focus only on winning. I worshiped people like football coach Vince Lombardi, revering him as the patron saint of conquest. So any time one of my victories was less than complete — or, God forbid, I actually lost — my sense of failure was absolute. And this always made me a sitting duck for self-pity — the handmaiden of John Barleycorn.

Joe C., my sponsor, picked up on this soon after we met. He gave me some good advice."Take the words 'success' and 'failure' out of your vocabulary. Replace them with 'honesty' and 'effort,'" he said.

I wasn't yet ready. I was an advertising hotshot who thought he knew more about competition than did Joe, an electrician at the time. So I continued my Type A behavior and reveled in constant conflict at home and on the job. But his words haunted me for years.

In time, I began to weary of the anger, resentment, and hate fostered by my competitive attitude. One day, another old-timer, Claude W., asked, "Why are you so afraid of losing? Don't you trust God?" Heatedly, I pointed out that, like him, I was in marketing and was paid to succeed.

His response had roots in the same stock Joe had planted years before: "Don't you know that success and failure share a common denominator?" He paused and then really let me have it."Both are temporary!"

His words have stood the test of time. They helped me to stay sober and to find joy in my chosen profession, with my family and among friends. I thank God, Joe, and Claude for teaching me this lesson in plenty of time to reap its rewards.

Jim M.
Escondido, California

Spiritual Agony

February 2001

Making an amends to the murderer of a precious friend was the most terrifying prospect — next to taking another drink — that I have faced in sobriety. But it also turned out to be the most liberating action I have ever taken sober and the opportunity for which I am most grateful.

My drinking career was short but intense, complete with downing eye-openers on hangover mornings, innumerable blackouts (including a few of the four-day-long, wake-up-in-another-country variety), two car accidents, and four stints in the psych ward, where I detoxed for what I pray was the last time. I was nineteen years old.

I have been sober now for almost two years, and I never cease to be amazed at how deeply the Promises come true for me as I incorporate the principles of our program into my life. However, the first six months of sobriety were enormously painful. I got little relief from the spiritual agony I was in, and, because I did not take the Steps, my compulsion to drink was not lifted.

One chilly October night, as I waited for a ride, shivering and half-heartedly participating in an after-the-meeting meeting, someone suggested that I pray the Third Step prayer and get to work on a Fourth Step. To put it mildly, I balked. I had read the Big Book and sat in enough meetings to know that taking inventory of my resentments — and forgiving those who had wronged me — would play large roles in working the Fourth and Fifth Steps. But because I was, in my mind, the epitome of an innocent victim, I saw no reason to forgive anyone, and I nursed my resentments as if my life depended upon keeping them alive.

Finally I had had enough. My spiritual agony was becoming unbearable. I didn't want to drink again, and without fail, every AA I met with a quality of sobriety I wanted had taken the Fourth and Fifth Steps thoroughly. As one of them put it: "If you want what I have, do what I do." So I sat down and wrote my Fourth Step.

Then in admitting my wrongs to another human being, I was able to see that my resentments had not just been eating my lunch; they had been ruling my life. The people for whom I burned with hatred didn't even know I hated them, and if they did, they probably wouldn't care. My anger was poisoning my soul, not theirs. I wanted to hurt them and was only hurting myself. It was as if I were swallowing rat poison and waiting for those I thought were rats to die. And I was truly surprised that it didn't work.

One especially difficult resentment was a reasonably justified one.

When I was a teenager, a dear friend was murdered. He had been an important part of my life and the closest thing I had to a father. When he died, I felt as if I had been dropped into a shark tank with an anvil tied to my foot. "Swim!" the whole world seemed to be saying, jeering at my confusion, loss, and pain.

His killer was found guilty, but insane, and sent to a state mental institution. Imagining the murderer in a paint-chipped ward full of drooling patients in straitjackets gave me some relief. At least she was locked up and in a terrible place, although that wasn't bad enough, of course. The only fitting justice for her was to be slowly tortured to death with my bare hands. And not even that would have satisfied me. I wanted the killer to hurt like I was hurting, and that just wasn't possible.

In the rooms of AA, I found a God of my own understanding, and, with his help, I was able to forgive the person who had caused me this deep pain. But forgiving is not forgetting, and the death of my friend occupied a lot of space in my mind and heart on a daily basis. Though I no longer burned with hatred, the killer was still living in my head rent-free.

I prayed for compassion and received it. One night I was struck with the realization of how lucky I am. All the mistakes I made when I was ill had been repaired to the best of my ability; none of them had been permanent and final. The agony of being responsible for someone else's death is a horrible thing. I learned that in the rooms of AA while listening to people whose drinking led to another's death, usually when they were behind the wheel of a car. There but for the grace of God went I. As an active alcoholic, I was a potential killer every day. That was the truth, and like all truth, it was hard to swallow. I also realized that when my friend's killer was restored to sanity through proper medication for her mental illness, an overwhelming and unamendable regret would be part of her life forever.

A few days after reaching eighteen months of sobriety, I knew that the time had come for me, with God's help, to do my best to set the situation right. I had learned in AA the power of forgiveness and the freedom it offers, both in being forgiven and extending it to others. I wanted that freedom.

My friend was dead; I could not change that. What I could do was make amends for selfishly nursing my resentment. I had burned much energy in useless anger and hatred, and the best way to set that right would be to do what I could to promote healing.

Taking a friend with more than a decade of sobriety, I went to visit the killer in the mental institution. I was clumsy and fumbled my words, but what came out was what was truly in my sober heart: "The person you killed was like a father to me. He meant the world to me. I loved him more than I can put into words. But I have come to a place where it's okay. I used to hate you for taking him away from me, but I don't anymore. I forgive you completely, I sincerely wish you all the best in your life, and I hope you keep getting better. I knew it would be good for me to come here to tell you that, and I hope it will help you to know that someone who loved him very much and was affected really hard by losing him has moved on and forgives you and it's okay."

Grateful that my voice didn't crack and that I didn't get sick from the butterflies dancing in my stomach, I took a deep breath and said a silent prayer of thanks. Then, I sat and watched as the human being in front of me expressed the most sincere sorrow and regret I have ever seen. It allowed me to make peace with my loss. Now I believe that mental illness had robbed this woman of the power of choice, and my friend had died because he was just in a bad place at a bad time.

As I walked down the sidewalk back to my car, I felt the deepest level of forgiveness I've ever known. A 500-pound weight was lifted from my shoulders. I felt free and cleansed. I had just found wings, and they were mine.

Holly H.
Huntsville, Alabama

The Mouth That Roared

August 2001

I always talked too much. Long before I picked up my first beer and long after I put down my last scotch, I talked too much. When I was afraid, I talked to hide my fear; when I felt inadequate, I talked to convince you that I was hip, slick, and cool; when I was in trouble, I talked in such convoluted circles that many times teachers or policemen or sergeants threw up their hands in defeat. I talked so damn much, I got good at it. Or so I thought.

But as my years of sobriety added up, I decided it was time to take a fearless and searching look at this character defect. It was then that I discovered something alarming about myself: in order to fill the air with my words, a lot of what I said was negative. In fact, many of my monologues were little more than verbal volleys against people, places, and things — from the President down to my in-laws, and including my friends and my fellow AAs.

One beautiful fall day, I had a moment of clarity as I was driving with my wife and another AA and his wife. The AA was someone I'd been sponsoring for years. He was also one of the few people who talked more than I did. As we drove along, I began to monitor what he was saying. Here's how his talking went that day: first, he presented the problem, then some dumb so-and-so's solution (which not only didn't work but made the situation worse), then his solution, followed by a series of events that proved his solution was the only successful one. When a new topic sprang forth, my pigeon would listen for a while — but not too long. Then he would begin his cycle all over again.

Listening to him — I mean really listening to what he was saying — opened my eyes (and my ears) to what I'd been doing all these years. As I listened to him, I heard myself. If you sponsor people, you'll never need a mirror.

As soon as I realized this, admitted I was powerless over my tongue, and took a fearless look at the defect, the solution came: if I only said positive things, I'd be talking half as much.

From that day in the car, I've tried to live by this simple edict. When I start bad-mouthing someone, I quickly curtail my tongue. I've gotten in a lot less trouble since then. (And since I've shared this with my pigeon, he has too.) Oh, I have slips. I revert to type. Before I know what I'm doing, I'll hold forth on so-and-so's latest debacle or so-and-so's program or marriage or whatever. We are not saints. I'll never get this idea down pat. But I'm a better person than I used to be.

The person I used to be is always waiting around the corner. If I close my eyes, I can see him. He's wearing a black leather jacket, smoking a butt, leaning with his back against a building and one knee bent. He's waiting for me to split a six-pack and join him in cussing and complaining and cutting down everything from his ex-boss and the Army to the church, academia, the government — and AA.

But when I close my lips to vicious talk, the old me gets tired of waiting around for someone to commiserate with him. When I say only positive things, the old me disappears. He flips his cigarette into the gutter, turns up the collar of his jacket, and walks away. He just doesn't want to hear it.

John Y.
Russell, Pennsylvania

A Remarkable Sensation

March 1997

I was one of those AA newcomers who chafed at the "God parts" of the Twelve Steps. I thought it was beneath my dignity to believe in God. As a budding alcoholic in my early twenties, I had become infatuated with existentialism, a philosophy that contemplates the role of the individual standing alone in an absurd world. Existentialism seemed to dignify my feelings of isolation and uniqueness and to impart a kind of tragic poignancy to the drunken impulsiveness I liked to think of as acts of free choice. When I entered Alcoholics Anonymous, I desperately wanted to stop drinking and to turn my life around, but I was pretty sure I didn't need the help of "God."

However, even during my first days in AA, I was wary of poking holes in the program, lest the whole fabric rip apart. I suspected that if I were to allow myself to make even one exception for myself — such as determining that I would ignore the God Steps — I might open myself to a justification to drink. Therefore, I determined to find a way to live with the whole AA program, including God.

But what did Step Three mean? "Made a decision to turn our will and our lives over to the care of God as we understood Him." How on earth did a person make such a decision? Turning my will and life over sounded like an enormously complicated procedure. And even if I could figure out how it was done, what would become of me if I complied? I worried that by following God's will, I'd end up doing something brave and self-sacrificing — and utterly repellent.

The "Twelve and Twelve" said that the only thing required to take Step Three was "a key called willingness." I thought I was willing. Imagining myself holding this elusive "key," I waited for transformation and felt nothing. The book also compared one's awareness of a higher power to electricity flowing, hidden and potent, through the circuits of a house. But I was unable either to feel the movement of this force or to find the switch that would activate it in my life.

The key finally turned, the electricity finally surged, in a way so quiet and simple I could never have consciously willed it.

At the time I got sober, I had been living with a man for several years. Our relationship had been in trouble for quite a while, and my new sobriety only aggravated our problems, for he felt threatened by my growing reliance on AA, and I was uncomfortable with his continued drinking. I would wake in the middle of the night and discover that he had not come home, and I would fly into a two-pronged panic that he had died in a terrible accident or that he was with someone else. I lay in bed with my eyes wide open, my heart racing until I heard his key in the lock.

One night began typically. I woke, realized he was not home, and felt the fear surface. Then something altogether different happened. I understood that I did not have to follow that route. Without even thinking about what I was doing, I said, not exactly to "God" but definitely not just to myself, "Whatever happens, let me accept it." Instantly a wave of calm washed over me. The panic evaporated. I knew from the core of my being that, because I was sober and was not going to drink over this situation, I was fine. I trusted — something. I fell asleep.

That was sixteen years ago. When I woke up the next morning, I knew I had taken Step Three at last and I was filled with joy. Step Three has continued to manifest in my life in ways that are ever more surprising and profound, for, as the "Twelve and Twelve" promises, "Once we have placed the key of willingness in the lock" and experienced that first opening of the door,"we find that we can always open it some more." Shortly after "turning it over" that night, I broke up with the man I was living with. A few years later I married a man I met in AA. I have stayed sober and continue to go to meetings.

And, interestingly enough, following a spiritual path has become increasingly essential to me. Contrary to my fear that taking Step Three would condemn me to a life of brave self-sacrifice, I find instead that it frees me to think and act as my truest self. My work, which is writing and leading wilderness trips, helps people explore the connection between nature and spirituality. In following this path, my own journey has flowed along several tributaries. Ultimately, however, the entire process comes down to Step Three: I stay sober and turn my will and life over to the care of God as I understand this wise and radiant entity which is manifested in my own soul.

There is an update to this story. One defect of character I battled for years was a bitter jealousy of other writers whom I perceived to be more successful than I. I had worked hard to let go of this chronic ache, but it continued to be easily provoked. A few weeks ago, I did a guided imagery session in which I saw the black, bitter bile of professional jealousy being removed from me by a kindly monkey, who placed it in the earth, where it dissolved and became harmless. A couple of days later my young stepson called to say that his first book had been accepted for publication. I waited for the grip of jealousy, but, astonishingly, felt nothing but happiness for his success.

The next day I reflected on this phenomenon as I drove along the highway in my car. I was thinking about how inner change seems to come only when we are truly ready for it. And then I heard, very clearly, a voice: Are you finally ready to let go and live your destiny?

An old, lingering part of me — that couldn't pass up an opportunity to bargain for what I want — rose up and I thought: Maybe if I say yes, I'll become a famous author.

Yes, I said to the voice.

No, it said. Are you ready to let go and give your life to God?

As often as my Higher Power had addressed itself to me directly in my years of sobriety, it had never before referred to itself as God. Certainly I had never called it that. The fact that it now did so shook me mightily. How could I argue?

Yes, I said simply. I'm ready.

I felt then a remarkable sensation. It was as if my entire body was being emptied of what it no longer needed and was instantly filled with something else. The sensation was of light and energy, a kind of tingling current moving through me.

Here was yet further evidence that AA's miracles can always deepen and crystallize if I don't drink, practice the Steps, and trust the process. As long as I am willing to do what I am called to do in any given moment and to abandon the effort to control the results of my actions, then I am following the path that my Higher Power — call it God, Good Orderly Direction, the soul, the life force, or anything else — has set out for me.

Trebbe J.
Thompson, Pennsylvania

Wait for the Pitch

March 2001

It was the summer of 1999, and in order to cover the costs of the October wedding my fiancée and I had planned, I was working as a maitre d', babysitting boozehounds in a fancy gin joint. The money was more than fair, but I hated the job.

I was in my sixth year of sobriety. I knew all about the "actor" noted in the Big Book and his desire to control the elements of production, I was familiar with the key of willingness, and I was aware of the nature of a determined and persistent trial. In my opinion, I had pinned the Third Step to the mat. Still, I suffered tremendous anxiety when I wondered how we were going to pay for our wedding, how I could stomach another night at that job, and how we were going to manage after we got married.

Deep in the throes of this apprehension, a friend who's well-placed in the corporate world offered me four free tickets to an afternoon Yankees game. They were playing my favorite team, the Tigers, and the seats were right behind their dugout, behind third base. It was just the break I needed and I gladly took the tickets. But consternation came on the heels of my acceptance.

None of my buddies could take an afternoon to loll at the ballpark with me. I was stuck with three great tickets, and I didn't know what to do with them. I resolved to turn them over to the One Who Has All Power. I got down on my knees and said I would trust him to figure out what to do with those tickets.

Riding the No. 5 train to Yankee Stadium, I sized up my prospects. Nobody felt right. I continued to place my trust in my Higher Power.

I encountered a man with two children, a boy and a girl, at the box office. Three baseball fans. Three tickets. I asked the dad if he wanted them. I couldn't accept any money (give freely what has been freely given), but I warned him and the kids that they'd be stuck with me for the afternoon. I promised to be on my best behavior, and politely declined his beer offer. A soda, I thought, would be fine.

I got what I came for. It was a tense contest. In a late inning, the Tigers put a man on first, and the next batter took off with the pitch. He lined the ball to right field, and the runner, who'd gotten a terrific jump, was rounding second. The Yankees' right fielder came up with the ball cleanly, but he rushed his throw to third. It landed in the coach's box, kicked off the railing in front of us, and caromed just over our heads. A vicious scramble ensued. The little boy got showered with beer, but his dad emerged with the ball. He handed it to his son, soaked but happy, the proud new owner of a Major League baseball.

A Yankees' beat writer led off his column the next day with that throwing error, the beer-drenched boy, and the dad who retrieved the ball. Reading the reporter's account, I realized that God was the one who brought all that together. It spread out from him, through me. A dad saved some money, a little boy won a souvenir, and a newspaper guy found a lead for his report, because I had trusted that God would show me how to act in this simple situation.

The Tigers, truly awful that year, beat the soon-to-be-World-Series-champion Yankees. Our wedding was a memorable, elegant event for which we received all the help that we needed. I have retired from gin mill work forever, God willing.

Today, I face difficulties that make distasteful jobs and the distribution of free tickets pale in comparison. My greatest challenges are before me. But my experience with the Third Step, even in the smallest matters, gives me the courage to meet whatever lies ahead, twenty-four hours at a time.

Pete P.
Manhattan, New York

SECTION 2

The Acid Test

"Then comes the acid test: can we stay sober, keep in emotional balance, and live to good purpose under all conditions?"

– Twelve Steps and Twelve Traditions, p. 88

As active alcoholics, we usually responded to a problem by drinking. Then we indulged in self-pity, resentment, fear — which didn't solve the problem. As sober AA members, we can choose a different path, as did the writers of these stories. Instead of giving up, or giving in to despair, these AAs were able to respond to life's challenges and stay sober — and "keep in emotional balance and live to good purpose."

It Was a Dark and Stormy Night

October 1998

Most of my life has been spent on the waters of various oceans. My father was a sea captain, and there were many sailors on my mother's side. Becoming a ship's captain was expected of me. The events I describe here took place in the spring of 1980. I was hired by a company in Anchorage, Alaska, to run their large fishing vessel, the Carole Jeane. I arrived in Seward that spring to pick up the vessel.

My dear friend Vic C. and I had then been in the Fellowship for several years. Vic had kept after me to take him with me on my next voyage in Alaskan waters, so, since he was good with marine engines, he became the engineer aboard the Carole Jeane. After a careful inspection of the vessel we concluded that it wasn't seaworthy, and we spent the next several weeks working on it, trying to get it into seaworthy condition. The owners were very anxious to get the vessel underway though I continually cautioned them about the unsafe condition of the ship.

Meanwhile, in Seward we gathered together several people with drinking problems; this was the start of the organized AA program here. (Today we have at least two well-attended meetings every day.)

The vessel was finally ready. My crew consisted of Vic the engineer, Bob the young cook,Tom the first mate, and myself. We left Seward on a stormy day and the ship's watches were set. Vic and the cook were one team, while Tom and I were on the other watch. The first few hours from port were uneventful. I really felt that we had the vessel under control and things were normal and the engines were operating well.

Then the weather worsened as evening approached, and after dinner I told Vic and the rest of the crew to get some sleep. I'd just returned from the engine room and things seemed to be okay and all systems were go. I picked up a cup of coffee in the galley.

I'd been at the wheel for about two hours when all of a sudden Bob the cook came running up the ladder to the bridge yelling,"We're on fire, we're on fire!" Black smoke followed him. I couldn't believe what was happening. The fire had had a huge start, and at first I didn't realize this. I stopped the vessel so we could concentrate on fighting the blaze. After a few futile minutes of this battle, I realized we were at the mercy of the fire and the vessel was quickly being destroyed. I sent out a May-day message — the vessel name, location, and the problem; fire at sea. I thought my transmission got out but there was no reply. The vessel's cargo consisted of two large gillnet boats plus 4,000 gallons of aviation gas in drums on deck. We also had 25,000 gallons of diesel fuel in tanks. Many tons of flammable material were stored in the vessel's cargo hold. I knew we had to abandon ship or we would surely die when the vessel exploded. Tom and Bob found survival suits. Since our liferaft and small boats were on fire, we had lost our main survival gear. The thought of spending a great deal of time in the extremely cold Arctic waters of the Gulf of Alaska was not very comforting. I instructed the men to throw overboard anything that would float. I crawled into my stateroom with a towel over my head to partially shield me from the toxic black smoke. Finally through touch and feel I found a survival suit which I later learned was already damaged by the fire and full of holes.

I can still see Vic jumping into the very cold sea wearing only a life jacket and everyday work clothes. His personal survival suit had been burned by the fire. As we swam away from the fire we found a styrofoam packing case and several timbers. Vic climbed in the packing case for protection from the cold, but the case filled with cold sea water and the situation worsened.

The seas were running from ten to twelve feet, and fog and darkness shut the visibility down to a few yards. Our situation was desperate and we knew it. The two young crew members were very frightened and soon became hysterical. These young men were sure they were going to die in these freezing Alaskan waters. Vic and I decided that the only way we could restore some sort of order and get our crew back to thinking about survival was to have an AA meeting! Can you imagine two members of the Fellowship of Alcoholics Anonymous having a meeting drifting in the Gulf of Alaska on a dark and stormy night, hanging onto a piece of styrofoam? Our two young crew members were spellbound; they stopped their ranting and raving and started to listen to Vic and I talking about how good our lives were and how fortunate we were to have found the AA program. Vic and I were actually laughing as we shared our sober adventures together.

As time passed, Vic became colder and colder, and we had to support his body and keep his head above water to keep him from drowning. After about three hours, a boat light appeared out of the murk. At this time the burning wreck was still afloat and about a third of a mile away. The rescue vessel started a search pattern that took another two hours before their lookout spotted us in the water. After they fished us out, more dead than alive, we began to warm up. Vic was delirious by now so he was wrapped in blankets. I climbed into the bunk with him and tried to transfer my body heat to him.

Our rescue vessel took us back to Seward where we were all hospitalized. Three of us were released the next day, but Vic remained in intensive care for several days because his temperature had been below normal for such a long period of time. Finally he too was released. Vic lived for three more years. He could never work at his old job again. He was never the same.

Vic C. was my inspiration and dear friend. He encouraged me and introduced me to the program of Alcoholics Anonymous. He was my sponsor.

Jack S.
Seward, Alaska

The Value of Life

June 2005

I am doing a life sentence in prison because of an alcohol-related accident, one that resulted in the death of an innocent man. So far, I have had several thousand days to re-evaluate my life.

When the shadows of my past were placed in the light, I was thankful for the "design for living" that the Twelve Steps provide. It helps me to handle the shock of who I was, who I am today, and who I want to be. But, even after ten years of sobriety, I find I am just scratching the surface. I have had some very painful moments of reflection on my life and on the actions and behavior that brought me where I am today.

Today, thankfully, a clear and sober mind provides me with the framework to lock my priorities in place. These priorities have become a part of what I consider imperative to the success of my life. But more importantly, they are imperative to the happiness and success of my family. Someone has said that the greatest gift we can give our family is peace of mind; I agree wholeheartedly.

However, once I think I have everything in place and the transformation into my new life is complete, something happens and I am reminded that I am a work in progress.

Three years ago, in my seventh year of sobriety and sixth year of incarceration, I thought I had finally got all my priorities straight. I couldn't have been more wrong.

I was talking to a good friend on the phone, and I brought up the fact that my youngest daughter, Shelly (not her real name), was turning six in a couple of weeks. I explained to him that I was very sad she didn't know what it was like to have a daddy at home. Up to that point, the only daddy that Shelly knew was the one she saw every now and again in a prison visiting room. When she was a baby, I knew I was going to prison for the loss of a man's life, so I memorized every single thing about her and hoped that she would recognize me when she saw me again.

As my friend and I talked, he recognized my despair and wanted to make Shelly's birthday better. He asked me what kinds of things she liked because he wanted to go out and buy her some presents for me. I sat there on the phone in silence because I didn't have a clue what my little girl liked or wanted. I couldn't talk anymore and hung up the phone and went to my bunk and cried. Here I thought I had made all the right changes to ensure my family's happiness, and I didn't know what to tell my friend about my own little girl. I had, once again, discovered that an important priority in my life was missing — not only with my youngest daughter, but with all of my children.

This provided me with the opportunity to make some necessary changes. Sure, it was tough to endure another failure, but in dealing with life on life's terms, I already knew it was going to be difficult at times.

Seven years after my last drink, I still had not become the person I wanted to be. But after weeks and weeks of asking questions and sharing laughs with my little girl, I am a whole lot closer to being that person.

I discovered that everything I thought really mattered no longer did. I found that the little things I took for granted on a daily basis were the things that meant the most. When the fog lifted, and I was standing alone in a strange land, I realized how clouded my thinking had been during my self-medicated haze. I found out, very quickly, that my family was waiting, with hope in their hearts, for the person they knew and loved to return.

As I continue to work the Steps, I write my goals and priorities in pencil, so I can erase them. This is not so I can sell myself short, but so I can strive for more ambitious outcomes. Recovery is a lifelong process; the moment I engrave in stone my blueprint for living, I'll rediscover and recover something that is paramount to the value of my life. And then I'll be looking for a new stone.

Although it is hard not to envy those of you who are free today and can hold your wife and children in your arms and tell them how much they mean to you, I am very thankful to AA and what it has done for my life. In recovery, my life truly does get better, day after day. Each setback I encounter is really just another opportunity in disguise. It is another chance for me to become a better human being. If life can get better for me within the walls of this prison, then I know it can get better for everyone.

Today, I share this Fellowship with recovering alcoholics all over the world who have taken the time to write me and touch my life in a positive way. AA is an amazing Fellowship filled with amazing people. I am constantly humbled by the wonder of it all.

Jeff P.
Blythe, California

Spiritual Coffee-making

August 2001

Recovering alcoholics and coffee seem to go hand in hand — or hand in mug. (If there isn't any coffee when we want it, life can seem very unmanageable!) The spiritual progress of my coffee experience shows how the Steps have helped me improve my relationship with my wife.

Early in my sobriety, I worked nights at the same job that I'd had for a few years. Often my wife would get up before me and start her day. Sometimes she'd be going off to work, sometimes she'd be getting the kids off to school, and other times she would be just doing things around the house. Some mornings, she'd make coffee, and other mornings she'd be content without it.

I would get up after she'd been up for a while and ask if the coffee had been made. Usually the answer was no. This would be cause for much discussion! I just couldn't understand why she wouldn't make the coffee and, if she didn't want it, just leave it for me when I got up. I didn't see how it would take that much effort to make a pot. After several of these discussions, I resolved that there was nothing that I could say that would make any difference anyway, so I wouldn't try to convince her that she should make coffee. I could see clearly that my cries were falling on deaf ears. So I'd get up and grudgingly make the coffee, and we'd sit down and have a cup or two.

Although I stopped mentioning this to my wife, I would often revisit the thought — i.e., the resentment. I knew I was powerless over the coffee being made before I got up, and I began to see the unmanageability of this issue in my life (Step One).

I knew I needed God's help and that he could do for me what I couldn't or wouldn't do for myself (Step Two). I also knew that I needed to take this to God and let him relieve me of my desire for things to be my way. When I prayed the Third Step Prayer, I disciplined myself to really listen to the words "relieve me of the bondage of self, that I may better do thy will. Take away my difficulties, that I may better do thy will." When I heard the words of this prayer, I knew that my difficulty wasn't having coffee ready for me when I got up in the morning. My difficulty was of my own making. This is evident when I am trying to get other people to do things the way I think is best — the way that would best suit my desires.

Next I had to see the selfishness in trying to arrange the show my way (Step Four). I saw this and admitted it to God and my fellows (Step Five). I was convinced that in order for God to remove my defects of character, I first needed to stop practicing my defects of character and doing what wasn't working (Step Six). Then I could humbly ask him for some guidance and direction to see how he could remove these shortcomings, and ask for what would work in this situation (Step Seven). The Seventh Step Prayer states: "I pray that you now remove from me every single defect of character that stands in the way of my usefulness to you and my fellows."

After a few years of sobriety, an opportunity came along for me to relocate to Omaha and work the day shift. As a day-shift person, I had a new routine that I followed every morning. I got up at 5:30 A.M. and made a pot of coffee. Then I showered, brushed my teeth, and got dressed while the coffee was perking. I poured two cups of coffee, one for my wife and one for myself, and while the coffee was cooling (my wife likes her coffee cooled down a little), I said my prayers and did my meditations (Step Eleven). Then my wife and I would have our coffee and conversation before I left for work (Steps Eight and Nine).

I've since moved back to rural Iowa and changed jobs. I still work the day shift and get up before my wife. I still have the coffee made and two cups poured each morning (Step Ten). I still allow time for my prayers and meditations while the coffee cools down. We still have our coffee and conversation each morning. This is as spiritual as life gets for me when I live as though I have had a spiritual awakening as the result of these Steps, and I practice these principles in all of my affairs (Step Twelve).

Last Sunday morning on the way to church with our four children, I mentioned this coffee experience to my wife. My insistence that the coffee be ready for me when I got up was several years ago now, and my wife said she barely remembered these episodes — or discussions as I like to call them. She was touched that I see having coffee with her as a spiritual experience.

I also shared this experience for the first time with my home group last Sunday night. It was a very moving experience that made my eyes leak. (I still have an ego and don't like to say that sharing this experience brought tears to my eyes.)

By the way, this reinforces the importance of a home group where each member can feel at ease sharing experience, strength, and hope. I need my home group to be a place where I can learn to practice the principles embodied in the Twelve Steps with other alcoholics. This sets in motion my willingness to practice these principles in all my affairs, including my home life.

Bill H.
Vinton, Iowa

Winners and Whiners

October 1994

I love the diversity of our Fellowship. I got sober in a small town blessed with three meetings a day, and I have come to appreciate that there are many kinds of meetings — the rough-and-rugged newcomer meetings, the philosophical middle-sobriety ones, and the living-in-the-solution old-timer meetings. I can usually inventory my feelings and needs, then choose the meeting that's right for me. What sometimes happens, however, is that I can selfishly forget which meeting is the right one for service.

I have three sober years now and during the past summer, life was a breeze. When life is easy, I usually assume it's God's way and I'm quite spiritual. But when I'm in emotional trouble, I assume life's a drag and that God's gone fishing. What I've had to figure out is that I can't figure anything out — that when life's a drag, it usually means I'm not living in accordance with the truth that life has its ups and downs. The most difficult part of this phase of my development seems to be my lack of compassion for my own physical and emotional hardships. I kick myself most when I'm down.

Last summer, everything was a snap. I had a terrific job, I was working through close friendships with people in the program, and I was staying in sound physical shape. Then this winter I injured my back, I lost my job, and I've been having a hard time connecting with people. I've been turning my woes over to God on a daily basis; I've been working the Steps; I've been attending lots of meetings; I've been working with my sponsor and sponsoring two great fellows — and yet I'm still living in fear and having physical, spiritual, and emotional blues. The idea comes easily to me that I'm not good enough or that I'm not lovable or that I deserve misery.

My life is so uncomfortable now, and there seems no sign of change, and yet I know from those around me that time takes time. My growth has always been slow and painful. I sometimes have to laugh when that phrase from the Promises is read: "sometimes quickly." But it helps me to remember that the phrase that follows is,"they will always materialize if we work for them."What I notice most is that I am not drinking — a miracle when I consider that people have gone out under similar circumstances — and that I am talking about my feelings. And I am well aware that alone I cannot solve my problems, but that with God and the Fellowship, I can keep growing and living.

So these days, I go to all the meetings. I work with newcomers at the rough-and-tumble meetings to remember what it was like when I got here; I go to the philosophical meetings because I need to hear how people are staying sober; and I go to the stay-in-the-solution meetings because I need to celebrate my sobriety and give myself a break. There are winners and whiners, and sometimes I seem to embody both. I am, as my friends remind me, a human being.

After three years, I'm finally arriving at the second half of the First Step: my life is unmanageable. (They say that if drinking won't bring you to your knees, sobriety will.) But I want to avow that through it all — and I'm always reminded that it hasn't been that long, it just seems long — the Fellowship of Alcoholics Anonymous has never failed me.

Gabby H.
Port Townsend, Washington

Faith in Full Flower

November 2003

Yesterday was my wedding day. I have been in this relationship for twenty years now, and the decision to finally tie the knot was prompted by the rapid physical decline of my wife's twenty-four-year-old granddaughter. She has cancer and is not expected to live more than a few weeks at best.

The hastily planned ceremony was held in her hospital room, with five generations of immediate family in attendance. A startled but good-naturedly cooperative social worker also got swept up in the celebration, and a camera was put in her hands to help record the event for posterity, with its light moments and poignant ones.

The vows and rings were exchanged at the foot of our granddaughter's bed, and her young son got to participate as the ring bearer. At one point, he had to crawl under the bed to retrieve my ring, which my nervous bride had dropped before she could get it on my hand.

After the ceremony, we served a simple cake purchased that morning, and a couple of bottles of sparkling apple cider to toast the marriage. For the toast, I asked my granddaughter to offer a few words. She spoke of how she sometimes felt neglected, and angry at Alcoholics Anonymous for all the time we spent at meetings when she was a child, but was grateful we were sober. She also told us she was glad still to be alive to witness the wedding we had put off for so long.

Somehow, it didn't seem strange to anyone there that the wedding was not held in a church, or a park, or someone's backyard. It seemed perfectly natural to bring together a family for a joyful occasion, even in the midst of preparing for a season of grief.

I tell you all this for a reason. Our book Twelve Steps and Twelve Traditions states that "well-grounded AAs seem to have the ability, by God's grace, to take these troubles in stride and turn them into demonstrations of faith."

I am not certain if I have accepted the fact that our granddaughter is about to die, but for some strange reason, I am not afraid. She has a strong faith in God, hopefully as a result of watching us grow spiritually in Alcoholics Anonymous. I believe that, if God ordains that her work is done, we should not try to keep her here. We need to show her that our willingness to accept his will does not apply just to the mundane things in life, but even to the death of a loved one.

When I was sober a year, my grandmother passed away, and I did not handle it very well. I made some mistakes that have yet to be rectified, and which cost me my relationship with my own mother. I now have many more years' experience trying to "practice these principles," and so hope to do things very differently this time.

Butch M.
San Diego, California

Epilogue: Everyone present agreed that our wedding day was our granddaughter's last "good" day. She passed from our sight and hearing six days later.

The Scariest Thing

June 2006

The scariest thing I ever did was get sober. Living without alcohol thrust me into a world as alien and threatening as a Martian landscape. For thirty years, the bottle had been my worst friend, my dearest enemy. It was my companion, my keeper, and its loss left me shaky and alone — and afraid. I was afraid of you. I was afraid of me. I was afraid of a God I wouldn't even acknowledge. And I was terrified I would drink again.

So I was very careful. Hugging my fragile sanity close, I moved gingerly through the days. Like a refugee crossing a swift stream, I felt for solid footing step by step. Away from home, I felt I had lost my skin. I saw scorn in every eye, rebuff in every gesture. In my apartment, I sat reading at my kitchen counter, although the open living room was a half-dozen steps away. Somehow, on the comfortable sofa I might relax, lose purpose, drink.

The group I joined saved my life, was my life, is totally integrated in my life today. I took my fear to meetings and sat mute, listening. For an hour, I was safe. For an hour, I had a haven among those whose fear had once been as great as my own. I did not give my fear away — they took it. They eased it from my grasp with hugs and laughter, with shared experience.

Slowly, I became less brittle. I found I need not die nor go crazy. I learned to live with the one I feared the most — myself. Since those days over a decade ago, I've had my life seriously threatened by an auto accident, then cancer. But nothing about death is quite as scary as the exhilarating terror of trying to accept life.

Barbara D.
Carlsbad, California

Barbara died on November 10, 2005. She'd been sober twenty-six years.

SECTION 3

Freedom From Self

". . . the alcoholic is an extreme example of self-will run riot . . ."

– Alcoholics Anonymous, p. 62

As active alcoholics, most of us are self-centered, and when we come into AA, our behavior can be still motivated by selfishness, self-seeking, self-pity, and self centered fear. As we stay sober, however, we get released from "the bondage of self," as the Big Book puts it. We no longer have to be at the center of the universe. We learn a little humility. We give up the idea that the world must always respond promptly to our demands. We cease trying to run the show — ours and everybody else's. We stop playing God— and it turns out there is relief and freedom in that.

Lonely at the Top

May 1991

When I first got sober fourteen years ago, I had no trouble finding a sponsor. Just about everyone in the group had been sober longer than I had, so all I had to do was find someone who was active and with whom I could relate. My first sponsor was a New York Bowery bum. I related to his low bottom because I too had taken alcoholism just about as far as one can and still survive. He had been sober for ten years when I came to AA, and at the time that seemed to me an eternity. Now, some years later I frequently am the person with the longest time at the meetings I attend.

My second sponsor told me, "The longer you are sober, the narrower the path." At two years' sobriety, I thought this was nonsense. There will come a day, I thought, on which everything will be clear, and I won't have difficulty with the program. I heard one old-timer who said when he was on a rampage, "It is lonely at the top."

Last year, our groups had three people with over twenty years of sobriety who died. In a small town, these people had been truly larger than life and we had depended greatly on them. My sponsor was one of those three. He was in great pain from rheumatoid arthritis, and he suffered from emphysema. After his wife died, he began to rely on me and other sponsees for physical as well as emotional help.

During that time I began to suffer panic attacks. I had been a mental and emotional disaster most of my life with several mental hospitalizations, including electric shock treatment when I was twenty-five, and although AA and God removed these extreme problems, even thinking that they might return was a great threat. One night after a meeting I talked to a newcomer who was having problems. Like anyone else who has stayed sober for a while, I knew things to say that would help him feel better. He told me that I had a wonderful program, and I went home depressed enough to think about suicide. It's lonely at the top.

I need sponsorship, and I especially needed it then. My sponsor was too sick to talk to me very often, and I just didn't want to burden him further. I began to look for another sponsor and ran up against the brick wall — the available pool of sponsors mostly had been sober for less time than I had been. I began to discover that being on top is not just lonely, it hurts. The next day I called up an alcoholic who had been sober a mere five years and asked him to be my sponsor, even though he was the pigeon of one of my pigeons. Like me he had recovered from severe mental problems, and I could relate to him. I also later asked someone with only three years in the program.

I believe that I have been far more teachable with the last two sponsors than I have ever been before. My new sponsor, just having finished a Fourth Step himself, encouraged me to work on one and to follow the section in Alcoholics Anonymous closely and carefully. I had done Fourth Steps before, but somehow had never been willing to follow instructions. It seemed to me, with my long-term sobriety, that I had better behave myself with a less experienced sponsor.

I certainly do not encourage using a sponsor who has just gotten sober, but after a year or so, anyone with a good program should be able to sponsor anyone else. I also do not subscribe to the statement that "the person who got up the earliest this morning has the most sobriety" — length of sobriety has brought me lasting benefits, and I have been more productive and comfortable than I ever dreamed I could be. But I still have no seniority — I am always one drink away from a drunk. I still need help, and sponsorship is an important part of the help that I need. I hear alcoholics bragging about how long their sponsor has been sober. It is good to remember that the length of sobriety is his, not theirs.

I hope that I no longer need a prestigious sponsor. I need help more than prestige. I am in AA for the long haul, and if I am to stay sober longer and longer, there are going to be fewer and fewer alcoholics who have been sober longer than I have been. I don't foresee outgrowing my need for help. I am good at talking to troubled alcoholics — I have sponsored a large number of people. But I have never mastered the art of self-sponsorship, and I doubt that

I ever will. What I need in a sponsor is one who is moving away from a drink, who actively works the Steps, and who is actively involved in the program on a daily basis. With those requirements, it is possible for me to find a large number of people with whom I relate. If a sponsor has to have fifteen-plus years, then I may be looking for some time. My sponsor who died said that, apart from staying sober, his greatest priority was to become an ordinary jerk. Having an ordinary sponsor helps me to achieve that noble goal.

S. C.
Harrisonburg, Virginia

Anonymity: A Day at a Time in the Real World

July 1995

When I was first sober and learning how to pronounce the word "anonymity," I thought it meant simply that we didn't use our last names at AA meetings. That was fine with me; I didn't particularly want the whole world to know I was an alcoholic. Because my drinking pattern included secret bingeing while I was alone, many of the people with whom I associated weren't aware of my alcoholism. They knew that something was wrong with me, but they didn't know what. So in early sobriety, I kept my mouth shut about my membership in AA.

Then, I went through the evangelist phase. I told everybody that I was a recovering alcoholic, whether they cared or not. I was more than a little proud of my sobriety. Anyone who raised an eyebrow in my direction heard all about alcoholism and recovery. What an expert I thought I was after just a few months of sobriety! I was disappointed when I realized that most people weren't interested in my discovery of the wheel. Patiently they heard me out, then turned the conversation to another topic.

After several years of sobriety, I finally reached a balance: I was comfortable talking about my alcoholism to interested people, but I had abandoned my effort to educate the entire state of Alaska. Then I got a job as a civilian dispatcher at a police department. During the interview for the job, no one asked me whether I had ever used drugs or drank to excess, so I didn't volunteer the information. I was prepared to answer the question honestly; however, I saw no reason to mention it if no one asked.

I'd been on the job for only a week when I overheard the sergeant talking on the telephone to headquarters. He was discussing the possibility of hiring another civilian for a job similar to mine: "She calls herself a recovering alcoholic. She says she has been sober for four years. She goes to the local high schools to speak to the kids about the dangers of drinking."

My heart stirred with excitement. Perhaps they were going to hire another program person to work with me! But then the sergeant paused, listening to the reply from his superior. He burst out laughing.

"That's right," I heard him say. "We don't need that kind around here."

I froze in my chair. A flush spread up my cheeks and across my forehead. "We don't need that kind," indeed! I was that kind! I could barely contain myself. With every bit of willpower I had, I forced myself to stay in the chair and keep typing. The urge was almost overwhelming to leap onto the desk and scream at that stupid sergeant: "I'm an alcoholic! Look at me! We do recover from this disease. See what a shining example of serenity and spirituality I am?"

As I stayed on working at the police department, I learned that the bad attitude many cops had about alcoholics was reinforced by their experiences in the field. They encountered us when our disease was at its worst. The cops responded to accidents, suicides, homicides, burglaries, episodes of domestic violence, and bar fights — and alcohol figured prominently in most of these. The cops dealt with the wreckage.

Once we alcoholics found recovery, the police rarely saw us. Suddenly we dropped from their lives, while others, still in the insanity of their disease, slid in to take our places. The cops had no time to wonder what had happened to those of us who disappeared. They were too busy trying to deal with the next crime, the next disturbance, the next accident, the next mess caused by a stillpracticing alcoholic.

The community of law enforcement officers was one more group of people to whom I owed amends. They, too, had been affected by my actions when I had been out practicing my alcoholism. It was painful for me to probe beyond my righteous anger at their apparent insensitivity to see that I had harmed them. But those police dealt with active alcoholism every day of their lives. To make amends for the stress I had caused police, for the pain I had inflicted, I couldn't just jump up on the table and tell them I was recovering. I had to show them.

I received plenty of practice in living the principles of the program while I was at work. When the police were angry, I had to forgive them for reacting to the insanity of active alcoholism. When they came back to the station from a child abuse call or a fatal car wreck, they were sometimes so angry they couldn't speak. Just beneath their anger, I saw the question in their eyes: "Why?"They wanted the carnage to stop. But the next day, another call would come in. Only the faces changed. I learned to admire the police for trying to bring alcoholics to a bottom, by making them face the destruction of their own and other's lives.

When things were quiet, when no one was angry, I began to speak about my past to some of the cops. Before I opened my mouth, however, I did a quick inventory, to determine whether my reasons for sharing were sound. I talked only when I sensed that what I had to say would help them. If my motives were self-seeking, in order to justify a lousy performance or to call attention to myself or to evoke pity, I kept quiet.

Those I shared with encouraged me in my recovery. One officer voiced a wish that more people would find the fellowship of Alcoholics Anonymous.

"We pass it on whenever someone reaches out," I told him."But they have to want recovery. When they are sick and tired of living that way, they find us.

When they ask for help, we try to be there for them."

Still, when the emergency calls flooded the police station, I had no time to talk about the program. The cops expected me to do my job efficiently, without excuses. Gradually, I became accepted as part of the team. It didn't matter to them what my past was, as long as I did my job to the best of my ability and didn't ask for special treatment.

Never while I worked at the police station did I broadcast the fact that I was a recovering alcoholic, but neither did I hide it. I valued my anonymity in that situation, not because I feared what the cops would think of me, but because I wanted to break it only when it might be of benefit to them. I made amends to the police by carrying the message through my actions that we do recover and go on to live responsible, productive, useful lives. The need to leap onto the table and tell them a thing or two disappeared. They found out who I was. And they accepted me.

Kit K.
Sterling, Alaska

We Get What We Get

October 2001

My local meetings are big on this spot-check reminder: you get what you get; it's what you do with it that counts.

From attending AA meetings in Iowa for the two years I spent in graduate school there, I brought home this question to add to my daily Tenth Step checklist: Am I still learning?

These two ideas help counter my abiding discontent with a job my old attitudes construe as being beneath me. Though I feel embarrassed telling new acquaintances what I do for a paycheck, the facts tell a different story.

Ten years sober, newly trained and degreed as a writer, I had plans for a blockbuster that would get my foot in the publishing door. But I needed to pay my bills. I bought a new suit to go to interviews in, came home that afternoon, got down on my knees, and prayed for God's will to be accomplished in my job search.

Not ten minutes later the phone rang. The local hospital, where I'd worked as a janitor between semesters at grad school, wanted to know if I could fill in for staff taking vacations. After a brief meeting with the supervisor, I came away with a permanent thirty-hour position that would pay my bills, provide health insurance, allow me time for meetings, and leave mornings free to write. I wasn't thrilled with the work, but the situation was . . . well, unbelievable. And remember: they called me.

Hey, I told myself, I'm sober, I've worked the Steps, I've got humility. I can do this a year, maybe two. And I'll use the new suit if I ever have to apply for a real job.

Fast-forward six years.

The new suit's been to two weddings. An overflowing cardboard carton of mostly unpublished manuscripts fills the bottom of my office closet. Among them are my Master's thesis, my résumé, and copies of applications to every publication within commuting distance and to a few that aren't.

After many schedule changes, several merit raises, ardent, fearful prayer, and incessant angry disputes among the committee members in my head, I am still mopping floors, getting to meetings, doing service work, sponsoring others, and writing in the morning. Recently, after requesting full-time hours, I was approached for running the department. Once again, they asked me. It's a real job, respectable, challenging, well paid, and a genuine contribution to a service-oriented organization. Best of all, you don't have to wear a suit to do it.

I had to tell them my heart is elsewhere. Showing up and doing the footwork is what I needed, not more responsibility. But I appreciated their consideration and might have a change of heart in the future.

I didn't lie. But the truth is that, working the lowest rung of the ladder has shown me some things about myself that I missed in several Fourth and Fifth

Steps: I struggle constantly with control and detachment. Childish grandiosity still goads me to make a moral issue of every little dispute. Some perverse instinct for unhappiness insists that I must be right. Not good management skills. But also not the emotional fiber necessary to handle a demanding job and also continue writing — which I'm determined to do.

The part of my job that always catches me off-guard, though, is the palpable jolt of pleasure I get from little ways to be helpful — to be of service — to others, for which they are so genuinely grateful. My dry or drinking mind, still alive and quacking, tries to avoid those calls, claiming that's not really my job. But the real litmus test for me is not letting fear and repugnance at close contact with very ill, decrepit, dying people sever my connection with my Higher Power. Whatever sense of victimization, injustice, absurdity, fraud, or bitter irony my sick mind thrived on drunk, my present circumstances force me to confront every workday as a shortcoming I've not yet mastered.

In early sobriety, I'd been through the loss of marriage, business, property, and money. So I thought I knew all about humility. But picture yourself down on your knees, cleaning vomit off the carpet in the ER waiting room. You glance up to see an old flame standing in the corner, cradling her new baby, and trying to figure out if that's really you. Test your ego-detector against that. Or say you run into the ex, who almost succeeded in taking everything away from you in that hostile divorce. She's coming out of the gift shop with an overpriced stuffed toy as you're sweating two bags of trash out the door. One of you has to give way. You should say something, right? But principles you espouse insist on civility. Maybe restraint of tongue is the best you can do.

So you know there's still work needed in that department.

Like the messes other people make, this is what I get at my job. It's what I get paid for. And it's taught me to view the mess other alcoholics make of their lives as a kind of job security.

Sure, I could compose a life more cinematic. That's easy. Give me a paycheck for the writing work I love — no more than I make as a janitor. I'm a humble guy after all. Or make me rich and famous, I don't care. Just leave everything else exactly the same: a loving marriage, fast friends, modest belongings, good health. This is what I tell God when I'm feeling resentful about what I've got.

But then I reach the end of another sober day and ask: So, am I still learning?

Oh, yes, indeed. And I promptly admit it's not all to my liking. But I go to meetings and remember well that, however crucial, getting sober wasn't to my liking either.

That casts the story in a different light. And I thank my Higher Power for giving me the time and determination it takes to stay sober; and also to write this next novel, the one that's going to send me over the top. There's this middle-aged guy, see, who everybody's given up on. But he's got this one really cool idea that . . .

Well, you get the picture.

Ernest S.
York Harbor, Maine

The Root of Our Troubles

December 1979

Many years ago, when I was just a small boy, filled with curiosity, I went to my father and asked him what heaven was like. Wisely, instead of trying to describe something no one really knows anything about, he asked me this question: "Suppose you were in the kitchen and found the last piece of a chocolate pie. What would you do?"

"Well, I love chocolate pie," I replied,"so I guess I would eat it." "But what if you knew your brother hadn't had a piece?"

I was trapped. Now, I could see where his questions were leading me, and this was not going to be what I wanted to hear.

"If you were in heaven," he said, "you would save that last piece of pie for your brother. That's what heaven is like. It's a world where we all share and think of others' needs before we think of our own."

Well, I decided right then and there that I wanted nothing to do with heaven if that was the way it was going to be. Even though a part of me understood how nice it would be if that degree of harmony was possible, another part of me just couldn't give up that last piece of pie. Looking back, I can see that I've spent enormous amounts of my time and energy arranging people, places, and things in order to get that piece of pie. And not until I nearly destroyed myself with alcohol could I see that my way wasn't the road to happiness after all.

Not long ago, in an AA discussion meeting, my sponsor was talking about self-centeredness. He quoted from the Big Book:"Selfishness — self-centeredness! That, we think, is the root of our troubles." My sponsor declared that all of us probably had that phrase underlined in our Big Books. Well, I didn't know if I had or not. Believe me, when I got home that night, I looked it up, and

what a relief! — I had it underlined in my book, too.

But at the time I underlined it, the real significance of the statement had not been clear to me. Sure, I could admit that on occasion I had been somewhat selfish — staying out all night, spending the grocery money on booze but it wasn't until I finally got around to doing my Fourth Step inventory that I could see how much self-centeredness had contributed to my failure at life. It was on every page of my inventory. I had created a whole universe centered around me and what I expected out of life. I was my own God; therefore, I really had no God. How miserable life was when I saw the world only through my own eyes! I was unable to reach out to others, and they were unable to reach me. The wonderful experience of peace of mind eluded me until I found the program of Alcoholics Anonymous. Self-centeredness is a poison to my emotional system. It frustrates my every effort toward a comfortable and happy existence. A terrible chain reaction begins. Fear sets in. Anger, resentment, and self-pity become my guiding forces. My only escape is to put this awful selfishness aside and become involved with the world around me.

Alcoholics Anonymous is the perfect solution for our selfishness. This program gives us a purpose and a vision of something much greater than self. We work with others daily. We are forced to become involved with the problems of the newcomer. As a result, our own problems just naturally pale in comparison. When I haven't been to a meeting in a while, simply talking to one of my friends always helps.

Discussion meetings are my favorite cures for reducing this magnified image I sometimes get of myself. There is a magical power that works around those tables. I can go to a meeting wound up tight as a drum, and about ten minutes into the meeting, I invariably begin to feel better. Whatever the problem was, it may still be there, but my attitude toward it has changed. Sometimes, the only place on earth that makes any sense to me is a meeting of Alcoholics Anonymous.

But old habits are hard to break. Occasionally, I still catch myself saying something like: "Why is this happening to me?" or "What is it ever going to take to finally make me happy?" Blinded by my selfishness, I perceive things that way. But in truth, I don't believe it takes anything to be happy. It is an inside job, something I choose, or refuse to choose, for myself. Circumstances outside myself have nothing whatever to do with it.

Anytime I feel that life isn't treating me right, and that everything is against me, then I'm trying to play God again. The longer I'm in this program, the more convinced I become that I really have no idea what's best for me. Who would have imagined that becoming an alcoholic would be something to be grateful for? But indeed I am. Had I not become an alcoholic, I would never have found this way of life that I have always wanted so desperately. My surrender to alcoholism was necessary to open my heart and mind to the healing love of God.

When I joined Alcoholics Anonymous, you told me that if I would walk with you, I would be a free man; that I would never have to drink again if I would only follow twelve simple Steps. But, you told me that in order to keep what I had found, I would have to give it away. I would have to work with others, putting their needs before my own. Sometimes, I don't feel like doing this. I'm still a very selfish person. But I know that if I want to remain sober and free, then these are the things I must do. "Above everything, we alcoholics must be rid of this selfishness. We must, or it kills us!"

I know that my life is no longer my own. My life now is in the hands of "a new Employer." Even though I still complain now and then about the working conditions and sometimes have trouble getting along with my fellow employees, it's a great improvement over the way things were when I was in charge. Although I sometimes take my sobriety for granted, I am never ungrateful for it.

Today, I still don't know that much about heaven, but I've learned some valuable lessons about life on earth. For so many years, I had always believed that the important thing was to be able to draw other people's attention toward myself. I felt I had to have this attention in order to establish my self-worth. This was my only means of security. Today, I know that the opposite is true. The real gift of love is to be able to give it to others. The ability to love can never be taken away from me, except by me. When I can get myself out of the way long enough to love another human being, it's the best feeling I know of. I guess you might say it's heavenly, just the way my dad described it many years ago.

B. S.
Dallas, Texas

Ready, Willing, and Almost Able

April 2000

In my second year sober, my sponsor suggested going back to karate because of the humility I could gain. The idea of going back to karate at forty, a discipline I had started at age twenty-four, was interesting. After all, I'd already earned my brown belt when I was still an active alcoholic. In fact,

I'd done a lot of things while I was still active, including finishing my master's degree, working for myself, smoking two packs of cigarettes a day, and staying in a dead-end relationship.

While I was studying karate, I earned the fourth of five belts in three years. During that time, I learned more than just karate: I also learned what it was like to belong, and gained a sense of self and confidence, all the while in a safe place.

In most karate classes, people sit in a long row across the studio (or "dojo") and are seated in order of their belt color: the beginners (the "white belts") are on the far side of the room, and the advanced students ("brown belts" or "black belts") are on the other side. The colors of promotion in different martial arts vary and in our school went as follows: white, orange, blue, purple, brown, and black. By the time I left karate (at age twenty-seven), I had earned my brown belt, and was sitting on the advanced side of the dojo.

I started again when I was thirty-five years old. My karate teacher welcomed me back with open arms and introduced me to everyone, since I'd been her student from so many years before. I was not allowed to wear my colored belt, however, because I had not trained in seven years. Nonetheless, my teacher seated me among the other brown belts. After a few months, I was ready to wear my belt. However, my teacher was not of the same mind, believing that I should train for a few more months before wearing my belt. I did not think that this was fair, so I showed her and quit.

Fortunately for me, I got sober two years later and started to reclaim my life. What made me hit bottom was being a pedestrian in a hit-and-run accident in a deserted part of the city where I live. It happened while I was in a drunken blackout. I was frightened and never felt so unsafe. At my first AA meeting, I heard the guy at the front of the room say "Sit back and relax; you are in a safe place." I felt safe. There are so many meetings in New York City; I have been to my fair share, but that particular meeting is still my home group, five years later.

During my first year I met my sponsor. She is a woman with so much grace and humility, it still astounds me. I started working the Steps with her.

My Fourth and Fifth Steps centered a lot around childhood — and childish — resentments, including at the top of the list, a resentment against my karate teacher for not promoting me as fast as I deserved (in my mind) to be promoted. My sponsor reminded me to include assets in this Fourth Step, and toward the end of this long list was a two-page chronicle of how this same karate teacher gave me strength, confidence, and a sense of self, at a time in my life when there was very little emotional support.

So, here I was, at age forty, ready to enter karate class again. My teacher was glad to have me back again and introduced me to her other students, positively glowing — wasn't it wonderful that I had been her student years earlier and isn't it great that I'm back again? When, exactly, was this humility my sponsor wanted for me supposed to kick in? I got my answer ten minutes later, when all the students went to sit down. I wasn't wearing my brown belt — after all, I was "humble." When I walked over to the advanced side of the room, the teacher gently told me that I had to sit with the beginners and wear no belt. I thought, "This is different than last time. It's also difficult, but it's certainly possible to sit over here for a few months, until I'm permitted to wear my belt again and sit with the advanced students."

I wore no belt and sat with the white belts for eleven months. What amazed me was that after the first three or four months, I began to accept that I was, indeed, in the right place. This time, I was not ready to wear my belt and I was willing to wait. But I was still relearning karate, still feeling stronger, and still feeling the spirituality which flowed in that room. The difference this time was coming to accept that just because I was not allowed to sit with the brown belts did not mean that I did not deserve to be back in karate class. I didn't know this when I was active. Looking back, it is all too apparent when I see how quickly I was willing to quit karate the second time around, although I loved that class, that school, and that teacher.

This was the gift of humility, taken from the Twelve Steps and brought into my karate school. The only two truly safe places I have encountered in my life were my karate classes and AA meetings. And now AA gave me back karate, because after a year, my karate teacher gave me a new brown belt and told me that I had earned the right to wear it.

The school closed one month after I received that new brown belt, with my karate teacher retiring, going after pursuits of her own. Had I not returned to the school when I did, I might have missed this chance to learn the little bit of humility which was offered to me (yes, and the brown belt, too: it's progress, not perfection).

Of all the things that had happened to me during sobriety, the school's closing just made me so clearly sad. Feeling so unhappy, but not talking about it, I finally blurted out in tears at an AA meeting that I had no karate school, and that it had provided me with such a safe haven and now it was gone. I didn't think about whether or not this was appropriate for AA, but I didn't think it would matter, because no one would really know what I was talking about anyway, other than to remind me that I did not have to drink over it. However, after the meeting ended, an AA member told me about his own karate school. I went to check it out. The people at the desk handed me an introductory pamphlet, explaining that the study of karate at their school would not simply focus on the physical aspects of karate, but would concentrate equally on the emotional and spiritual aspects. This sounded very familiar.

I signed up for this school and explained that, although I had learned a slightly different type of karate, I had, after all, earned my brown belt; I hoped they were going to take that into consideration. They said that was fine, and gave me my uniform — complete with its white beginners' belt.

Elizabeth B.
Manhattan, New York

Thoughts on Step Seven*

August 1955

Time after time during my seven years of AA sobriety I have recognized a character defect and have asked God to remove it and He hasn't done it. I have asked why, and for an answer have been driven to an ever more careful consideration of Step Seven. Here I encounter the crucial word "humbly." If I really want a shortcoming removed I am to ask humbly — that is to say, in humility.

What is humility? It became one of the really vital words in my new AA vocabulary, but just exactly what did it mean?

During my first year or so, humility to me meant an absence of pride. "You've got to be cut down to size," an old-timer remarked, and I flared in resentment. Even while protesting, though, I had a hunch he was right, and it soon grew into a conviction. Getting humility was going to be a laborious grinding-down process, a grim, bumpy business of getting rid of pride.

This would mean a reversal of the way I'd been living, and thinking. All my life I'd been given to understand that to have no pride was contemptible. The strongest of all the pleas about my drinking (and in the end the least effective) was: "Have you no pride?" Pride of self and of family, of school, of business or professional affiliation, of social and fraternal contacts, of parents, children, and sweethearts, of prejudices and of locality, of possessions and of physical attributes, of nationality, intelligence quotient and creed — these I had been encouraged by a pride-puffed world to esteem as the highest values. Now I was told they were excess baggage, to get rid of them and be "cut down to size."

The job was slow, and even this long after is only fairly begun. Sometimes I wearied of it, and asked testily what it had to do with staying sober on any given day. But as the humbling stone of truth ground deeper I saw more and more clearly what it had to do with sobriety. Whenever one of my uncountable prides was touched I'd flare in resentment. And prideful resentment, AA's accumulated centuries of collective sobriety was trying to teach me, is an almost certain prelude to a drunk.

The first to go, and one of the hardest of all, was head-of-family, bigbossaround-the-house, or breadwinner pride. During all my drinking I had "prided myself " — literally — on being a consistent provider. I lost no opportunity to toot the theme on trumpet and cornet and beat it out in Morse code on the tom-toms. I was a damn good provider: let all realize this and pay homage.

As is so often the case, circumstances gave me sound help in getting rid of this pride. All in the same year, the industry I'd served for twenty years bounced me out of a job, and my wife of fifteen years, by legal force, tossed me out of my position as head of the family. And now, mind you, I was sober! I had a choice. I could hang on to my pride and enter into an angry war to win back lost prestige. The Big Book warned me against that path: ". . .the rage and the brainstorm are not for us."

Or I could ask "humbly" that my shortcomings be removed. That way I would have to accept good-naturedly the fact that my family and profession could get along perfectly well without me. I just wasn't as important a property as, all this time, I had thought. If they wanted none of me I could no longer, as of old, bully them into line. I'd just have to let them go their ways, and seek other company — AA company.

Before the cutting-to-size approach to humility was ended — or perhaps I should say before it ceased being predominant, as I doubt if it ever entirely ends — the rough diamond of my bumptiousness had had a number of irregularities ground smooth, or at least a little smoother, on the AA wheel. Every kind of "background" pride — physical or mental, social or ethnic, professional or geographic — tended to wither before the fact, clearly demonstrated at every meeting, that men and women completely lacking in these once-important attributes, possessed something of incalculably greater value to me. They knew how to live, and soberly. The more humbly I was willing to listen and learn from them, the more I gained (for from nothing at all to just a little is nevertheless a gain) in humility.

"Who do you think you are?"

This blunt question has the power to snap me back to a saner notion of my relationships to the universe and to other people, every time I seriously ask it for myself. It helps me to an understanding of my "size." Who am I? I'm one of two billion, 500 million people currently trying to make out an existence on the planet. I don't suppose I'm much more valuable to the Creator than any one of the others.

Nevertheless He has accorded me some very special favors. I shouldn't really be here at all. I'm here on borrowed time, on probation. For I'm alcoholic, enjoying an arrestment of a fatal disease. This certainly gives me no license to push people around, or get annoyed with them or rail at them for not being other than as they are. My proper attitude, AA has tried to leach me, is one of simple thankfulness that I'm still around. Perhaps I might even show a little appreciation of that circumstance, in terms of helpfulness. During the times when I'm thinking along these lines I have the feeling that I'm about down to size, and I'm more comfortable.

As the days have rolled into years, I've come to see that there's another and more wonderful aspect of humility than the negative one of getting rid of pride. It's a mistake to regard the search for humility as just the destruction of a prideful shell. When a chick is born the main event is the arrival on the earth of a new kind of life. In the excitement of this fact, the smashing of the shell is all but forgotten. I think our efforts to learn to ask humbly, that is, to attain humility, may be something like that. Certainly there was a period in the hatching when, from the chick's point of view, life must have seemed nothing but an interminable pecking away at an almost impenetrable shell. But finally it breaks, and he's free.

Might it not be a little bit so with us? In recent years I have felt unmistakably the stirring within me of a new and finer and entirely different kind of life. Possibilities for action within this universe have opened up . . . possibilities I hadn't even dreamed of before. May not we, too, know a new freedom once we're broken out of our shells of fears and fixed ideas, of prejudice and pride? Step Seven will always be to me the humility step. But humility means a little different thing to me, as an older member, than it did when I was brand new. It isn't all shell-smashing now; new life is stirring.

In the actual taking of Step Seven an unexpected dividend comes to the earnest applicant. When we really ask, as the Step suggests,"humbly," our major character defect, pride, is already on the way to being removed.

J. E.
Bronxville, New York

*Originally, this article was run without a title, as part of a series called "Twelve Steps and the Older Member."

It Works at Work

June 2000

A frustrating morning at work drove me to a noon AA meeting where I was called on to share. I unloaded my frustration of working with people who cared only for themselves. A coworker had (I thought) intentionally misled me about the location of a business meeting where, as a trainee, I was to observe him facilitate. This, I thought, was my big chance and he seemed intent on elbowing me out of the limelight. Four years of both college and sobriety had resulted in an unfinished degree and the title of clerk. No matter how hard I worked, nothing seemed to make a difference in either my income or my title. I was ambitious and hardworking but with no direction. I repeatedly asked my sponsor when I would know what direction I should take at work. His response was always, "Just show up and be of service."

After I concluded my whining, Joe D. was called on. He looked at me and said, "Debbie, no one was happier than I was that you worked the Steps. Now why don't you try working the Traditions? Start with the first one."

It was explained to me that to put our common welfare first, I would have to put myself second. Tradition One meant "putting ourselves to the side and working for the greater good."This was not what I expected to hear, but I had run out of ideas and became willing to try doing it differently.

It didn't take long for me to realize that in order to consider the common welfare of my work group, I had to be willing to let go of my resentments toward them, specifically toward my coworker. I had to look for my part in the situation because I knew by this time that people didn't usually avoid me without good reason. I remembered that a couple of times at a meeting which my coworker was leading, I had fired some of my sarcastic-but-funny comments at his expense. The group laughed but I remembered the look in his eyes. No wonder he was avoiding me! He couldn't control what was coming out of my mouth.

I had to clean up my side of the street with him and did so by telling him that I was both aware of and sorry for what I had done and in the future I would make every effort to support rather than embarrass him. I asked him if there was anything I could do to be of service to him. He didn't jump at my offer.

A few weeks later I saw an opportunity to be of service, and I asked him if he'd like me to assist with the design of a presentation layout for the training course he was preparing. It was an important project and one that he had put a great deal of time and effort into. He accepted my offer. This time, I had a different motive than before, designing to meet the needs of the presenter and the audience instead of my own desire to be paid more or singled out for praise. As the design began to take shape, so did my attitudes about my job. I began to experience the true satisfaction of being a worker among workers.

I found that I had an opportunity to help make something that fostered confidence rather than panic in the presenters. I even found opportunities to apply humor into the presentation, not the wicked kind that hurts but the witty kind that can help people feel good.

The week prior to the Big Event, my coworker asked me to accompany him because, as he put it,"I will have more confidence if I know you are there to help if anything goes wrong with the presentation." Imagine that.

As I worked the First Tradition to the best of my ability, I noticed a sense of well-being at work and an increased interest in others. It had never occurred to me before that the results of working the Traditions might be the same as working the Steps.

And the effect of Tradition One continues to amaze me. A few months after the Big Event, my coworker's wife entered the AA Fellowship for the first time. The combination of relief, gratitude, and awe at the power of the AA program washed over me when I realized that my behavior outside of AA could affect, either positively or negatively, a newcomer who had not yet entered our doors. What would they have thought of this program if I had not cleaned up my side of the street and worked Tradition One? Thank God we will never know because my coworker's wife liked what she saw, wanted what we had, and has just celebrated two years of sobriety. It is my privilege to be her sponsor.

What about my career and the title that I had been so anxious to attain? It comes as no surprise to me that my current job is to identify areas of need in organizations and then design information systems that will meet those needs. As for my job title, it will probably change when I complete my degree, somewhere around June 2001. Imagine that.

Debra M.
Richland, Washington

Simple Program

July 1980

Around the tables, slowly and with love, my AA teachers have done wonders with and for me. Long ago, I lost depression because of AA.

Now, that is a marvelous character defect to lose! As days float joyously by, with or without problems, the AA program continues to be fresh and delightful.

Early in the program, I found "ego deflation at depth" to be a goal toward which I would have to struggle, perhaps for as long as I breathed. Everywhere I turned in the Steps, I was faced with my pride. I had to battle — and continue to battle — to get off the center of the universe. I have not let this fight interfere with the beauty of living in sobriety. Rather, it keeps me steadily attuned to the importance of regular and frequent attendance at meetings.

There has been some improvement in the deflation department, I realized the other day. I no longer have to count the stars at night to make sure they are all out there and in their proper places. And so it is with supervising tides, sunrises, and the flow of rivers on either side of the continental divide, along with many other tasks of which I have been relieved.

Not being concerned with these details anymore, I now have latitude to work on more personal items such as lying, procrastination, indecision, lust, remorse, guilt, and so forth. As a result, the quality of life keeps improving. I complete each day knowing that — even if I no longer have much time to spare from meetings,Twelfth Step calls, family obligations, etc. — somehow, the universe is being cared for. What relief one can get from this simple program!

Anonymous

SECTION 4

A Program of Action

> *"It is easy to let up on the spiritual program of action and rest on our laurels. We are headed for trouble if we do, for alcohol is a subtle foe. We are not cured of alcoholism. What we really have is a daily reprieve contingent on the maintenance of our spiritual condition."*
>
> – Alcoholics Anonymous, p. 85

Saying that AA is a program of action is perhaps another way of saying it's a program of solutions. Of course we have problems — all human beings do — but we've been given a practical toolkit to help us stay sober in the face of all sorts of challenges. We take action by going to meetings and giving service, by putting the Steps to work in our lives, by reaching out to our fellow AA members, by healing relationships with family and friends, and by connecting with a higher power of our understanding. In these ways, we begin to look for solutions rather than focusing on problems and find we can live peacefully, happily, and to good purpose in the world.

A Benchmark in Sobriety

September 1991

When I arrived at the Eighth and Ninth Steps, I found I had an unusual amends to make. I needed to make amends to the entire town I grew up in, for various acts of juvenile delinquency. There was no way of finding individual firemen, policemen, or citizens I may have involved or harmed twenty years before. But I still wanted to make amends in some way.

I first tried writing a letter to the local newspaper, outlining my transgressions of the past, and declaring that I wanted to apologize to the town. The editor refused to publish my letter, saying that such a letter might actually encourage other young people to misbehave.

So I turned the whole thing over to my Higher Power and went on about the business of living in sobriety.

One day, after about a year in the program, I sat down on a park bench to rest. It occurred to me that someone ought to paint the bench, spruce it up. I thought about doing it myself, but I realized I would need a whole bagful of tools, besides the paint, to do a good job. It was too much for me to deal with. So I turned it over to my Higher Power.

Another year had gone by when I sat on another bench in another park and I thought,"Somebody ought to paint this bench!" I realized that over the preceding year I had acquired most of the tools I would need. All I needed to buy was some paint and some brushes.

I bought the needed supplies, assembled my tools, put them all in a large shopping bag, and began to paint park benches. I took it one day at a time, painting one bench at a time.

Over a period of three years I painted about thirty benches in three parks. Some of the benches were getting tough use and those I painted twice. I used a rasp to smooth out coarse edges and sandpaper to roughen the surface of the smooth, weatherworn boards so they would take the paint. I did a priming coat and another day a finishing coat. It took about four hours' work altogether to do one bench.

I want to say that I enjoyed the work. It wasn't drudgery for me. I was outdoors, in the parks, out in the sun and the wind, listening to the birds, watching the squirrels, and sometimes interacting with people in the park.

I never told anyone, outside of AA, that I was doing this to make amends. I just said that it needed doing and I enjoyed doing it. Some people asked if this was required court-ordered community service, and I said, "No, I'm just a volunteer."

Then came a day, after about three years, when it occurred to me that I was done. I had made my amends to the town. I didn't have to do it anymore.

Several years have passed. I still use those parks as a place to sit and rest. Occasionally I see a bench that needs painting and I remember the work I did. But I don't do it anymore. Now the town does it.

If you can't figure out how to make amends, just turn it over to your Higher Power. In time, there will be an answer, there will be a way.

Jack A.
Montclair, New Jersey

Dropout

September 1977

It was summertime, and I was stretched out in a lounge chair in my backyard. Not more than a schoolyard away, members of my home group were animatedly entering their AA meeting hall.

A twinge of guilt grabbed me, as I tried to avoid, for the umpteenth time, witnessing this happy scene of which I should have been a part. A momentary longing to join my fellow AA members asserted itself but was quickly dismissed.

Fifteen years before, I was privileged to be a charter member of that group, the greatest of all groups. (Isn't everyone's home group the greatest?) Now, here I was playing Russian roulette with my sobriety. I had not been an active member of my group for more than three years and had almost completely stopped going to meetings.

I became ungrateful, complacent, and irresponsible. How quickly it can happen! "Do I have to continue going to all those meetings, after so many years of sobriety?" I asked myself. Smug over my longevity, I thought I had reached a saturation point in learning how to stay sober. From two meetings to one to zero can happen so swiftly when our thinking becomes distorted by ingratitude.

I became an AA dropout, optimistically pointing to those who stay sober on their own. But, as we know only too well, the do-it-yourselfers have never entered the wonderful world of AA, so consequently they would not have the withdrawal blahs, as I did.

Much of my time now was being devoted to other activities. These were valuable in themselves, but they were divorcing me from my AA activities, which simmered down to conferences, breakfasts, and retreats, but no regular meetings. Soon, there was a resurgence of ego, a feeling that I no longer needed AA. I'd ever be grateful — oh yeah — but I'd go it alone.

Defects of character began to reappear. Some of my actions became excruciatingly embarrassing. When you punch a hole in a wall and you're sober, how do you explain it? Guilty conscience, maybe? And when you cover the damage with a Serenity Prayer from a Grapevine cover, you need to go all the way back to Step Two.

Needless to say, I was treading on thin ice. Aware of this, I accelerated my attendance at special AA events (though I still took part in no regular meeting activity). I was fearful of stretching my umbilical cord of AA security too far. Special events in AA definitely have their place. They're the answer for the alcoholic who has just sobered up and asks, "What am I going to do with all that time on my hands?" But the meeting is where it really is at, and your home group is the hub of all your AA action.

In fifteen years of sobriety, you find a lot of AA friends and acquaintances, and I renewed these friendships sporadically while attending the special events. The warmth of the longtime friendships had cooled a little. Fellow AA members, the finest and most dedicated associates I've ever known, were polite and congenial. Yet I thought I detected an estrangement, not intentional, I'm sure, but discernible. It had crept into our relationship while I wallowed in my absenteeism from regular meetings.

Surely, my abbreviated AA program was headed for a crisis. Then one day I ran into a friend who tendered me an invitation designed to get me going to meetings again. I was intimidated, in a sense; he was a former pro football player, a six-foot-four-inch, 255-pound end. I thanked him for the invitation, made excuses to break up the confrontation, and promised him I'd think it over (big deal).

After considerable deliberation that night, I finally headed for the meeting. Making that decision was like breaking through a brick wall. It seems that alcoholics are always breaking through walls of some kind.

Arriving at the meeting hall, I hesitated outside. My emotions were similar to those I experienced the night of my introduction to AA. It was quite a while before I could feel a part of that meeting, and several weeks passed before I was brave enough to crash through the barrier and attend my home group again.

My mental blocks were unwarranted. The members of the group where my sponsor-via-invitation was serving as secretary, as well as my home group members, were most gracious in welcoming me back. So I embarked upon another quest for continuous sobriety (how grateful I am that it was not interrupted), with a firm resolve that I would never again take an AA leave of absence.

It has been more than three years since my return to AA activity, and I've never been happier in Alcoholics Anonymous. I firmly believe that our happiness in this program is commensurate with our activity or lack of it. I go to at least three meetings every week. It was my privilege to sponsor a man shortly after my return to activity. I'm certain I would have had to turn him over to someone else had I not resumed working the program as it should be worked.

Together, my Higher Power and I have aided Clay to an active career of unbroken sobriety. He's done a great job, not only with his own program, but in helping others, and that's the name of the game.

A lot of wonderful things have happened to me since my AA rejuvenation. I've been privileged to be secretary to a new group, a group chairman often, and cosponsor a few times. Sponsorship, I think, is our biggest dividend. Seeing a family rehabilitated, the kids smiling again, makes the effort all worthwhile.

I still continue my extra AA activity, the special events, but I recognize them now for what they are — the gravy, not the meat.

If there was one major symptom that led to my inactivity and near tragedy, it was a loss of gratitude. I forgot to be grateful for the wonderful gift of sobriety, forgetting also that one of the best ways to express that gratitude is to pass on the program. Making the AA scene regularly assures us of an opportunity to carry out our mandate to assist suffering alcoholics.

E. B.
Newbury, Ohio

Think Small

March 1979

I think I have just learned something about humility. This puzzling word has bothered me ever since I came into AA just over a year ago. An old-timer said at a meeting that to him humility was truth, and I have just discovered some truths about myself that are humbling and yet give me a great sense of freedom.

The past few weeks, my thoughts have been pretty negative. I've been trying to live up to my own impossible standards, and I've been feeling very sorry for myself because I fall so short of them. But it sometimes seems necessary to think negative in order to get positive.

I am aware, for instance, that I am not and never have been a gourmet cook; but with the help of my Higher Power, whom I choose to call God, and with a healthy assist from Betty Crocker, I can feed myself and my family. I cannot clean the house in one day; but I can straighten up the kitchen and make the beds.

I cannot be a wise and tender counselor to my three teenagers and one almost-teenager; but I can point out that if they don't do their homework, they are not likely to pass the course; then, I can let them know that, pass or fail, I will still love them. I cannot always be a loving spouse and cheerful companion to my husband; but I can tell him how much more my life means to me because he is in it.

I cannot give anyone the precious gift of sobriety; but I can listen to a newcomer's problems and tell her how it works for me. I cannot teach a religion class; but I can share my spiritual experiences when it seems appropriate to do so.

I cannot do great things; but I can finish the things I start.

I cannot write a book about recovering from alcoholism; but I can tell other AAs about a new insight that has made my life more manageable by leading me to let go of some old ideas. And thank God, these things that I can do today are enough.

A. B.
Lombard, Illinois

What Will I Get Out of It?

December 2003

When I first got sober, I wanted to keep AA and all that went with it in a neat little corner of my life. I thought meetings were just for keeping me sober. I never thought that I would make it to the Twelfth Step, where I would be "practicing these principles in all my affairs." However, it wasn't long before what I experienced in the Fellowship started to seep into other areas of my life. At first, these were disturbing encounters, but I gradually saw there was much to be learned and applied.

A few months sober, I began to feel very alone and disconnected when I went to my faith community on Sunday. Nothing had changed at church, but I was changing inside. I compared my uplifted spirits and the aura of excitement in an AA meeting to the drabness I perceived in church. (Today I would probably call that drabness peaceful, but I had no tolerance for peace in early sobriety.) I compared the way I saw our congregation leave after the service to the way my AA meetings broke up: in church, we turned and filed out of our pews with little conversation, whereas in AA, we held hands, prayed, and talked to one another at length before leaving the meeting room. I was feeling lonelier each time I went to church.

One particular Sunday, I left the service sad and full of self-pity, feeling disconnected from my fellow worshippers. With all of my newfound, early sobriety "wisdom," I mounted my mental soapbox and launched several hours of alcoholic, obsessive thinking. You know the kind — where your mind picks an idea and chews on it from every angle until it's unrecognizable. By that evening, I had convinced myself that attending church was worthless and vowed never to return. Luckily, I had a husband who expected me to attend with him each week, so I was back at church the following Sunday. In the meantime, I made myself and my family pretty miserable.

Back in AA, I was blessed with a good dose of healthy fear about relapse and was doing everything my sponsor told me to do. I became the coffee maker at my home group, and sometimes served as a greeter, shaking hands and welcoming people as they came in. I baked cakes and cookies to share with my AA friends. The more service I did, the more people I met. The more people I knew, the more conversations I had at meetings. I felt more and more as if I belonged to AA.

Meanwhile, back in church, I decided to apply the same principle: if it worked in AA, why wouldn't it work in church? I became more active, volunteering as a religious education instructor. I enjoyed that, so I branched out into Youth Ministry and joined other committees. The more service I did, the more people I met. The more people I knew, the more conversations I had in church. I felt more and more as if I belonged to my congregation.

Could it be that I was working the Twelfth Step, "practicing these principles in all my affairs?" The greatest wonder of it all was how happy, joyous, and free I had become when I attended Sunday celebration at my church. Gone were my negativity and critical thoughts about the people around me. No longer did I spend Sunday afternoons sulking about not being spiritually fed by the morning service. And the people were suddenly so much friendlier! Or could it be me? It seemed that I was reaping what I sowed in every situation I entered.

Then, around my fourth year of sobriety, I found a spiritual advisor to help me with my prayer life because I wanted to work the Eleventh Step. Although she wasn't a member of AA, she was a friend of the Fellowship and I trusted her completely. After one of our meetings, when we were discussing a group prayer experience we had attended, I commented, "I didn't get much out of it." She became very agitated and said how sick she was of people saying that. "It's not what you get out of it, it's what you bring into it," she stated emphatically. (Here was a person outside of AA who truly understood the importance of ego deflation at depth.) Was I ever shocked! I was expecting some gentle spiritual nurturing, and I felt as if I had just been smacked. I guess I needed that smack to wake me up and help me remember that my experience of worship in my faith community had changed when I started bringing something to it, and how my connection to AA had grown when I brought more to that. Here was an opportunity to go to another level in my sobriety.

At that time, I was finding meetings somewhat burdensome: it seemed as if the same people told the same stories over and over again. Thinking that I was safely sober, I questioned the importance of allotting precious blocks of time to meetings each week. Instead, I could be out living my new, wonderfully sober life. I see now that I could have been headed down the road to relapse. I suddenly thought about how much I owed the Fellowship of AA. It was always there for me when I needed it. Perhaps on the days when I felt complacent about going to a meeting because I thought I was spiritually fit, I was supposed to help another suffering alcoholic by being available at a meeting. It could be that my spiritual advisor was right: it was more important that I bring something to AA rather than simply take from it.

That was a turning point in my sobriety. Instead of always going to a meeting to feel good, there were more and more times when I went to a meeting to do good. Right about that time, a newly sober woman asked me to be her sponsor. I was wondering why no one had asked me yet! I have had the privilege of watching her grow through the past six years. She has even made me a grand sponsor. What joy! In addition to sponsoring her and a number of other women, I have been able to share my experience, strength, and hope with hundreds, maybe even thousands, of recovering alcoholics inside and outside meetings. This wonderful weaving of AA into every area of my life is a far cry from the way I started my sobriety. I also know that it is bringing me closer to aligning my will with my Higher Power's will for me. Thanks to AA, I am living a healthier, integrated life, by "practicing these principles in all my affairs."

Anne S.
Albany, New York

Made Direct Amends

June 1990

"No, never! I'm willing to make amends to everyone on my list, but not to her. Not to Janice. Not after the terrible things she said to me. She called me a gold digger! She tried to turn her father and sisters and brother against me! As far as I'm concerned, she owes me an amends!"

As I finished my hostile outburst, my sponsor smiled sweetly with her exasperating, all-knowing look. "You may not be ready to make amends now," she said. "But there will come a time when you want to make amends to Janice.

When you are spiritually ready, your Higher Power will find the right time and place. You'll make your amends, and you will feel wonderful. I promise you, it will happen."

I didn't believe her. I couldn't imagine why I would ever make amends to a person who had insulted and offended me. Janice lived a thousand miles away and that was as close as I wanted her to come.

At thirty, Janice was my husband's oldest daughter. She had suffered terribly when her mother suddenly died of a cerebral hemorrhage. Her grief was so intense that she wrung a promise from her father never to remarry and to keep the family home exactly as her mother had left it. She was a devoted (although bossy) sister to her younger siblings. Talented, educated, and beautiful, she was the mother of an adopted son and a devoted member of her church.

I was told that she had many fine qualities, but no matter. She didn't like me and I didn't like her. She took her father's marriage as a breach of promise and vowed never to forgive him or me. When I tried to win her over, she angrily blamed me for alienating her from her family. She wouldn't listen to my drunk apologies and belligerent fuming. She didn't understand that, as a newlywed, I needed time (and plenty of alcohol) to adjust to my new status. It was all her fault! Then, somewhere during the last seven years of my drinking, she stopped telephoning. All communication between Janice and her family stopped.

But my sponsor was right. The time would come when I could hardly wait to make my amends. Making those amends would show the power of Step Nine to heal old wounds and unite loved ones.

By 1986, no one had seen or talked to Janice for almost seven years. She had stopped telephoning her father or the sister and brother who still lived with us. She never tried to contact her other sister, married and living in another state. Instead, she held on tightly to her grudges.

It was a family of grudge-holders. Her grandfather had gone to his grave without speaking to his brother for over thirty years. Her grandmother had refused to speak to her son's ex-wife for over twenty. If you offended once, you were never forgiven. Old slights were recalled and thrown in your face. No one in the family knew how to say, "I'm sorry." No one ever admitted he or she might be wrong.

Into this family I came — a practicing alcoholic on the final, downward plunge. I added my own flaming resentments to the troubles. I covered up my excesses by blaming the family. I drank the alcoholic's bitter brew of anger, resentment, and bewildering despair. In the end, I alienated my stepfamily completely.

That stepfamily was the primary target of my Eighth Step. I was two years sober when I wrote my list and made those first, difficult, direct amends. With newfound humility and dignity, I recognized my part in the angry scenes and hostile home atmosphere. I admitted my mistakes, as best I remembered them. I said those unfamiliar words, "I'm sorry," and I asked for forgiveness. I told each person what I was doing to turn my life around and promised that I would try my best not to offend again. I never mentioned the other person's behavior; I kept to my side of the street.

My husband and my stepchildren were astonished. No one had ever talked to them that way. No one had ever admitted his or her own weakness or failings before. The pattern of blame, excuses, and grudge-holding had left no room for human error or compassion. Miraculously, everyone accepted my amends with grace and good will. But the real miracle was that they began to realize that they could do the same thing toward those whom they had offended. Making my amends set an example in human relations that would be invaluable in the tragic years ahead.

As I saw and felt the healing power of Step Nine, I began to sense true peace of mind. I began to feel right with the world and right with myself. As I crossed off the names on my Eighth Step list and made my amends to each person, I felt stronger, more secure, more in harmony with myself and others. But something in me kept telling me I had more work to do. I looked at my list again and realized that Janice's name wasn't even on it. I had totally blanked her out of my mind — and out of my recovery.

As I reviewed my drinking behavior, I saw my motives more clearly. I had interfered between Janice and her father. I had contributed wholeheartedly to family arguments. I had purposely alienated Janice — to keep her from intruding into my life and to protect my right to drink as I wished. She had reacted with hurt anger, which let me justify my own self-serving actions. Seeing my own motives so clearly helped me understand the emotional and psychological stress my disease had created.

Now I wanted more than anything to clear away my guilt. I had reached the point my sponsor talked about: the point of spiritual readiness to work Step Nine completely. Now those thousand miles seemed like an impenetrable distance. I asked my Higher Power to help me find a way to make direct amends.

That summer, my husband and I went on vacation to Lake Havasu, Arizona. Soaring desert temperatures became too hot to endure. As we searched the map for a place to cool off, we realized that Southern California was only a one-day drive away. Janice lived near Los Angeles. We telephoned ahead to ask whether our visit would be welcome. Surprisingly, Janice seemed pleased. I now believe that she was as sick of grudges and bitter memories as we were.

Our visit turned out to be a delightful success. For everyone, it was time to bury the past and start over. On the final day of our visit, I asked Janice if I could speak to her privately. In a very sweet and loving manner, she listened while I explained about my disease and how it had affected our relationship. I told her about AA and how the Fellowship was helping me change my life. And I assured her that I would do everything possible to bring the two sides of our family back together. She paused for a few moments, then hugged me warmly and said, "I think what you're doing is wonderful, and I'm proud of you. Now maybe we can be friends."With those words, the past was gone. We could begin again.

For the next two years, family relationships healed. Janice and her father forgave each other and telephoned frequently. Her brother and his wife and children spent two vacations with Janice's family. Her younger sister moved to California and lived with Janice for six months. Although our relationship was cordial, it wasn't the kind of warm, supportive relationship I enjoyed with my AA friends. But I was happy that we were at least speaking.

Then, in January 1988, Janice telephoned to tell us awful news. She had ovarian cancer. At that moment, our friendship changed. Janice asked for my support, and I was completely willing to give everything I had to help her.

During the next twelve months, Janice endured two surgeries and eight chemotherapies. She lost her long, thick hair. She lost weight and muscle. She lost the socially active life she loved. But she never lost her faith. She was an inspiration to me, and I to her. Through the grace of my Higher Power and the lessons I have learned in AA, I was able to share my experience, strength, and hope — and help Janice keep a positive, faith-filled trust.

Janice's family rallied around her. Old grudges were forgotten. She and I talked at least twice a week, every week for twelve anxious months. Her brother talked to her as much, or more, than I did. Her sisters prayed, and they gave as much support and encouragement as they could. My husband and I sent cards and flowers whenever she went into the hospital. We drove our motor home out to California twice and camped out on the street in front of her house. When Janice was joyfully pronounced "cured," we drove out a third time to celebrate.

Warm, loving, bubbling with life, Janice talked about the future the same way a starving person talks about food. She longed for life, for happiness, for wellness. But six months later, she was dead. A reccurrence in the lower intestine. Colostomy. More chemotherapy. Wasting away. Finally, peace.

I still don't understand the terrible grief I feel. But I understand this: because of the spiritual power of Step Nine, I have no regrets where Janice is concerned. The family that wept together in that flower-laden church would not have been there if Step Nine had not worked its healing magic. Making amends started a chain reaction of forgiveness that changed a whole family.

As my sponsor promised me years ago, I learned more from that one amends — the one I swore I'd never make — than from any other person or event in my recovery.

Carol S.
Albuquerque, New Mexico

The Work at Hand

March 1988

There's the chirrup of a sparrow, the rhythmic tak-tak-tak of a woodpecker, and a low, steady roar from the Interstate. I have stopped work for a moment to rest my racing brain and listen to the silence. When I stop thinking, I find that it isn't silent at all. Even out here, miles from the city, life makes itself heard.

Tony and I are building a small studio for a friend. The pay isn't much, not enough to float my sinking financial ship, but it's work. We often must work one day at a time, uncertain of what job will come next. If I don't worry, and just do each job as well as possible, it's enough. Of the little money we do earn, ten percent goes in payments to people or institutions we have cheated or harmed in the past. By following this and a few other simple suggestions, we stay sober and live fairly decent lives.

It was a big, fat surprise to me to realize that I was alcoholic. One month, I was foreman of a construction crew for one of the more prestigious builders in my area. My wife taught school. We were buying a home, a "fixer-upper" with great potential. Sure, I drank a wee bit too much, but our lives were fine, on the surface. One month later, my wife was gone, I was unemployed, and I was an admitted alcoholic.

Tony takes a last drink of coffee, looks at his watch, and tells me it's time to return to work. We are digging footings by hand. It's hard work in this rocky mountain soil, but like many things that are hard or unpleasant, it has compensations. It keeps us strong, and we get to work out-of-doors.

When my wife moved out, I called a mutual friend, hoping that with her acting as a go-between, we could coax her back home. But Lois did not want to talk about how to get my wife to return. She directed the conversation again and again to drinking. She told tales of her own drinking, and I soon responded with tales of my own. She had seen me in my cups, and I could not convince her that I was a social drinker. As we talked, it became clear to me that most of my problems had been caused by my drinking.

She invited me to a meeting that afternoon, and I accepted. She cautioned that people in meetings introduced themselves as alcoholics. Could I say I was an alcoholic? I didn't know then what it meant to be an alcoholic, but I would have claimed I was a zebra if it would help me not to hurt so much.

"I'm James. I'm an alcoholic."

I said it. The A word. I've said it many times since, and I have not had to drink since that September Sunday.

My brain still works overtime. A large part of my recovery has been in learning how not to listen to myself. When my wife moved out, we decided that I should stay in the house we had been buying together, paying her when I could for her relatively small portion of the downpayment. With the job I had then, such payments would be difficult, but not impossible. A few weeks later, the builder I had worked many years for began to hire subcontractors exclusively. I was out of work.

Then began the darkest hours I've ever faced. In addition to inescapable remorse over having driven my wife away, I woke each day to the likelihood of financial ruin. While unopened bills gathered dust, my brain worried over my situation in dozens of variations. Worse, I slipped into the forever syndrome: I was doomed — I always had been, I always would be.

"Don't think about it," Gentleman Jim told me. In the group I attend regularly there are a lot of Jims, so they get nicknames. Jim says that he was nicknamed "Gentleman" because he wasn't one. I was explaining to him how I thought the Fourth Step worked psychologically. After all, I had already been in Alcoholics Anonymous for more than six weeks, and

I had been writing my Fourth Step for more than a week. Surely I was an expert.

"Just do it," he repeated."Don't think about it."

"But that's why we have brains," I argued. "To help us understand the world, and make decisions based on that."

"Your best understanding got you to Alcoholics Anonymous," Jim reminded me. "Just do what's in front of you, don't think, don't drink, and go to meetings."

"Don't think, eh?"

"Don't think!"

I thought about that. Eventually, I began to see that what I had called thinking was not thinking at all but a kind of squirrel cage of doubt and worry that went around the same issues over and over and always brought me back where I had started.

When my life was very good, I thought it should be still better. I looked for angles. I told myself the world was an accident of physics, and therefore each person was free to take as much as he could. For a long time that attitude was moderated by the people I loved. I moderated my grandiose ambitions enough to include them. As my stinking thinking progressed, I cared less and less for myself and almost nothing for the people who were closest to me.

My conscience could not be stilled. I tried myself again and again, and was found guilty each time. I was worthless, aimless, unkind. Each hurt to others joined the slush fund of self-conviction inside me. I began to drink more to cover that darkness inside. My brain continued its fevered pace, trying to find a way out of the endless loop I had created.

I was a successful employee partly because I tried to keep pace with my spinning brain. At night, every night, I could take my medicine. The daily drinking that had begun a few years before as a beer or two to relax me had become a daily six-pack, and sometimes more. Occasionally, I moderated with wine — often a quart or more each night.

A few months before she left, my wife came home from working late and walked onto the front porch where I sat. I was drinking wine from a quart mason jar. The remainder of a half-gallon was in the refrigerator.

"Are you drinking again?" she asked.

"Yeah. But just a couple. I've really started to get my drinking under control." "But you drink every night," she said."Every night you drink."

I thought about that briefly and arrived at the only logical solution. Without answering her, I walked to the back porch, where I could drink in peace.

Tony leans on his shovel and looks at me funny. "Are you thinking about your wife again?" he asks.

"Well, yeah, a little," I answer. I feel like I used to feel when my mother would discover five or six missing cinnamon rolls from the dessert tray.

"James," Tony screeches. "I miss my M-16. You should have seen her. Her name was Janice, and she was a beauty. I lost her. Woe, woe."Tony is a Vietnam vet. When he came to Alcoholics Anonymous, his sick thinking was of the terrors of war. He often nails me like this when I get caught up.

While I still drank, there was one conclusion my thinking was not allowed to arrive at. Since the conclusion I avoided — that I drank too much — was at the heart of every problem, my thinking became circular and dishonest. It was like living in a house with a black hole in the corner of each room. No matter where I went, there was a black hole. When I drank enough, the holes went away. By the time I began receiving help, my brain did not work well anymore.

I also ached with guilt and remorse. I was not a big-time operator, but I had hurt the people who cared most for me.

"Well," said Bicycle Bob. "None of us got here because we sang too loud in church." In meetings, people were sharing their own shortcomings with the group, often to uproarious laughter. It was easier to admit my own faults in such an atmosphere."You're as sick as you are secret," we say, and my goal now is to be an open book.

I am not a saint, as the long list of people I have hurt demonstrates, but I am working on that list, making amends whenever and wherever they come up.

Probably my most satisfying amends was to my high school music teacher. Twenty-five years ago, he loaned me one of his own music books. Out of laziness or greed, I never returned the book. I have moved about fifteen times in the years since, and have owned and lost a lot of books. I always packed and carried that one book with me, though, through all the houses and cities. I had stopped studying music, and the book was merely baggage.

After a little detective work, I found his address and returned the book with a letter of apology. When I did, I became a little freer. I had one less dark secret to think about.

Tony tells me that it's time to go home. I have been in outer space again, thinking, thinking. When I get caught up in that squirrel cage I often make mistakes. Today I was lucky. Tony must have been maintaining good ground control. The footing trenches are squarely cut and right where they are supposed to be. I hear the low roar from the Interstate again. I have landed safely back on earth.

I have fired accidental physics as the creator of my world and replaced it with my own understanding of a loving God. As long as I practice the principles which keep me close to him, and do as well as I can the work he puts in front of me to do, I will get what I need. I no longer have to think about how my life should go. This brings peace.

I am still strapped financially. I have not found work that pays as well as the job I had when I was still drinking. My wife is now my ex-wife, and is already remarried. Those are pretty tough cookies. What I have now is a growing faith that my life is being directed by a Power greater than myself.

It's only when I stop thinking about it, stop trying to run the show, that my life may become as God intends. I still have consequences of my drinking years to live through. While that is happening, my job is to be, like these trenches, squarely cut and right where I am supposed to be. When I do stop thinking about it, I know that I have finally come home.

James L.
Tucson, Arizona

Take My Advice - I'm Not Using It

May 1997

I was feeling rather depressed and called my sponsor and found her in a similar mood. I said, "What shall I do?" At first she said, "I don't know. If you figure it out call me back." Then because she is a loving person, a good friend, and has a terrific grasp of the AA program, she shifted into sponsorship gear and told me to do the following:

Wear life like a loose garment.

Don't take myself so seriously.

Count my blessings.

Find another alcoholic to work with.

Read the Big Book and go to a meeting.

Then she laughed and said,"Take my advice — I'm not using it."

I called one of my sponsees, and she was also in a negative frame of mind. I addressed her problem and suggested one through five listed above. She said she had a sponsee in a melancholy mood. I proposed that I and my sponsor, she and her sponsee could form a singing group called The Depressions and sing the blues. She was not amused.

Later in the day my sponsor dropped by with another friend for coffee — and what a change! She'd made a Twelfth Step call and taken another alcoholic to a detox. They recounted how she looked like ten miles of bad road, was ill and full of fear and remorse. Suddenly we were all full of gratitude and laughing at the insanity of self-pity and self-imposed depression. We remembered all the pain and confusion of our early days in Alcoholics Anonymous.

The simplicity of this program never changes — what works is constant: trust in God, clean house, and work with others.

Terry B.
Concord, California

SECTION 5

OUTGOING LOVE

"Lord, make me a channel of thy peace –
that where there is hatred, I may bring love –
that where there is wrong, I may bring the spirit of forgiveness –
that where there is discord, I may bring harmony –
that where there is error, I may bring truth –
that where there is doubt, I may bring faith –
that where there is despair, I may bring hope –
that where there are shadows, I may bring light –
that where there is sadness, I may bring joy.
Lord, grant that I may seek rather to comfort than to be comforted –
to understand, than to be understood –
to love, than to be loved.
For it is by self-forgetting that one finds.
It is by forgiving that one is forgiven.
It is by dying that one awakens to Eternal Life."

– Twelve Steps and Twelve Traditions, p. 99

Most of us will never perfectly achieve the ideals expressed in this prayer, commonly known as the St. Francis Prayer. But the stories in this section show that when we are able to practice outgoing love, we can, in the words of one writer, "start being open to all the gifts the AA life can bring."

Put Aside Anger

July 1965

It seemed to me once that the great trick in learning to live the AA way of life was to put aside anger. I think now that it's rather a matter of learning to love — and serve. I dimly see these days that there is no freedom from a messy inner landscape of greeds and compulsions until somehow, someway, we are focused on the miraculous fact that we are given the world and all the people in't to love. Shakespeare's Miranda, pure-of-heart if ever anyone was, concluded from the sight of one very ordinary young man that it was a "brave new world" that lay in store for her beyond Prospero's island. I think we see fairly soon in AA that there is to be for us indeed a brave new world — if we will just walk out and live in it with love. Ah, but it's not so easy to do. There is time needed, and that changing we call growth, and a great deal of help from fellow AAs and from our Higher Power.

Almost all of the time the way to live in outgoing love eludes me. So, perhaps, it is not out of the way to keep on working meanwhile against the negative things. I continue to try to eliminate anger. Surely this comes before the birth of love?

As it happened, anger was the first character defect that I came to acknowledge that I possess. It rose to the surface for inspection within a matter of weeks after my entrance into the Fellowship. I could see, and dislike seeing, that I went regularly into rages, and between times lived in a kind of cold suspicion of everybody. (How can you love such unsatisfactory people as the world presents: mean, self-serving, fickle?)

When at last I saw how prone I was to childish tantrums (oh yes, dressed up with adult language and force) I saw — and my heart sank — that it was I who was mean, self-serving, and fickle. It was I who was unloveable, and therefore I who was the cause of my anger at life.

This insight was a shock; I felt that the center of my being had been bombed out. But it was a profitable emptiness for once. I've been in rages since, although less frequently, and have forgotten myself with frustration at friends and kin I don't know how many times, but I am never far away these days from the restorative sense that charity begins at home: I must love (accept) myself, at least, so as to be able to stop being angry and start being open to all the gifts the AA life can bring.

Anonymous

Some Long-time Views

March 1984

May a special shaft of serenity shine upon some alcoholic who thought up and shared that pleasant word "long-timer" instead of "old-timer." I must reciprocate with some long-time views!

One month ago, I shared my thirty-fifth AA birthday on a Sunday night at a meeting in Rondebosch. There was no banquet, no bells, not even a birthday cake. The only concession was a tape recording of the talk. But in that hall, love cascaded over me and poured over my wife, Jessie, who, on one unforgettable morning in 1947, beseeched me to write to New York for help when I was dying of alcoholism at the age of twenty-five here in South Africa.

There was no phone number to call; regular meetings were to materialize much later; there was no local box to write to furtively, no material proof in the form of a sponsor to show my trembling vision that AA worked. That was the way it was. That was the way it had to be — for me. I was perpetually terrified, a mass of fluctuating suspicions, so thin-skinned and painfully sensitive to the slightest vibrations of authority that if there had been a nearby AA group or central office, I doubt if I would have made contact with it.

For me at that time, it had to be done through the quiet power of the written word, initiated by Bobby, at the AA General Service Office in New

York, and embossed by Ann M., Bill, and Bob, who sent such love in so many letters over many years. As compulsively as I used to drink, I now felt a celestial obsession with AA sobriety, and my exhilaration forced me to write all over the States for any crumbs that they could spare. They sent me whole cakes of indescribable mental richness, iced with humility, laughter, and alcoholic love. After groups were formed here, Bill W.'s guidance often saved us from calamity.

One day, the Big Book (it had somehow been overlooked) was placed in my hands at five in the afternoon, when I arrived home from work. As I recollect, I had been undergoing the early pangs of "monotonous" sobriety that we often feel around our fifth month in AA, when we haven't a clue about the program. There was a cup of tea on the kitchen table, ready. Next to the steaming cup was the book, in a navy blue cover — Alcoholics Anonymous, 1948 printing.

I finished reading this masterpiece at six the following morning. The tea, now cold, remained untouched; the ashtray, empty. I hadn't had time to loosen my tie or remove my jacket. Only once did I leave the table; then, the book went with me to the bathroom. It was the greatest, most artistically crafted journal of recovery, and it still is. I was spellbound by the majesty of the wording, the delicacy of the suggestions, catering to the individuality of each alcoholic. At last, this whole venture made sense! For me, the essence of it lay in the second paragraph on page 164: "He will show you how to create the Fellowship you crave."

I have read this beloved book over and over. It still uplifts, inspires, and guides. Through the years, I have read thousands of books and pamphlets, but the Big Book is still the superstar. The love flowing from its pages encourages me to keep the blade of my sobriety ever sharp and gleaming, to cut through all the ignorance and terror that surround still-suffering alcoholics. When their tears dry and the pain recedes, I see in their eyes the image of God, always illuminating the Fellowship of which I am a part, thanks to him and to all of you.

P. O.
Wynberg, South Africa

An Equal-Opportunity Deplorer

March 1983

I came to AA because I was "sick and tired of being sick and tired." By not drinking and by going to a lot of meetings, I achieved the sort of dryness that made it unnecessary to drink — and also unnecessary to discard most of my old ideas and conceptions. I picked a "sponsor" who supported that system.

I was free to not drink, not work well at my job, be as irritating as a hangnail in a pickle factory, and deplore the antics of any and all groups in and out of AA. I was an equal-opportunity deplorer: I felt particular animosity toward motorcyclists, bankrupts, homosexuals, people who took any kind of drug, divorced people, liberals, ad nauseam. But for some reason, even with all these people to roundly deprecate and feel superior to, I wasn't happy. As a matter of fact, I was very unhappy. I drew some kind of perverse enjoyment from my misery.

I changed jobs and cities. Through a series of adroit and somewhat sneaky moves, my Higher Power let me wind up in an AA group consisting of people who worked hard on the program. With the help of a solid sponsor, I went to work on the Steps, all twelve, in the manner and in the order in which they are explained in the Big Book.

Almost without realizing it, I was losing enough fear and gaining enough faith to feel okay. It was no longer a case of just being sick and tired of being sick and tired; my life changed to such an extent that I was no longer afraid to be "happy, joyous, and free." As I worked through the Steps slowly and sometimes hesitantly, my attitudes, my self-image, my relationships with other human beings — virtually everything in my life — changed. I no longer wanted to run out in front of everybody and holler,"Follow me!"

I found that people outside the program could be as loving and sharing as those inside. Times changed; life changed; and people in the program began asking me to sponsor them. God saw to it that I was kept busy; for that reason, I needed to help new people recover as quickly as they were able, so I would have time for others who asked.

Along with that, He began to set me straight on some of those old ideas. I ran into one "bankrupt" who didn't even know that he was. Since joining AA, he has worked off, without legal bankruptcy, tens of thousands of dollars of indebtedness. One by one, they came into my life: liberals, young people, hippies, Bill and his Harley-Davidson, state employees, a tenured professor, gays, and lately, when God so elected, one member who must have some medication to correct his brain so that he will be able to function.

I ask God each morning, "Please take care of . . . ," and I name them all. Each night, I thank him for taking care of every person on the list, which has grown to eighty-five names. Just who is sponsoring whom is in God's hands after a while.

I have learned to begin each of these sponsorships with the statement: "I am willing to love you, to accept you just as you are. I will not judge you nor expect you to do anything just to please me. There are no qualifications on this love. I will never suggest that you do anything I have not done. If you want what people with good sobriety have, then you will do what they have done — the Twelve Steps of this program."

I ask each one to call me anytime he feels like it, to share joys as well as problems. In the past, I sometimes made the mistake of saying,"Call me when you have a problem."The upshot was that I was "teaching" my friends to have problems so they would have a reason to call. Now, we talk over the good and the indifferent as well as the occasional off-the-program days. I have driven my car many a mile, quietly and slowly covering the back roads, sharing and talking, laughing and sometimes crying. These are times of building trust, learning to share, gaining the faith to be "happy, joyous, and free." I gain insights into myself and learn how God wants me to broaden my horizons in the program. So many things from so many sources have aided me in reaching into myself and others that I cannot always pinpoint just when and where a particular truth occurred to me. However, I want to share what I consider to be two key concepts. The first is that as long as I am acting in a loving and caring manner, I am not responsible for how others react. This frees me from pleasing people at my own emotional expense. The second concept is, I feel, the clearest basis for sharing our insides with another: feelings are neither right nor wrong. It is what we do with our feelings that we should concentrate on.

Through sponsorship, the program taught me, slowly and ever so gently, to love and be loved. It taught me to touch, to walk by a friend and pat him or her on the head and say,"That's just in case nobody gave you a pat on the head today." I learned the value of saying,"You're okay," with a hug. I learned the fun and joy of being childlike, of being able to laugh and enjoy life. I learned life. As I share what I know of the program and am willing to learn from those with whom I share, I find a deeper and more rewarding contact with God. My understanding changes and broadens through wider and wider exposure to many different kinds of people from varied backgrounds. The one common element that runs through all these relationships is the strong desire to stay sober and to go beyond sobriety to full-fledged recovery.

R. M.
Temple, Texas

As Unique As Ham and Eggs

June 2000

Thirty-two years ago, in april 1968, I lay on my bed in a fetal position. I was told by a doctor that he didn't think I'd live through the night. That was where my alcoholism took me. Today this seventy-twoyear-old black man would like to share with you where my sobriety, one day at a time, has taken me.

I woke up this morning at about four A.M. The electric clock was blinking at me because the electricity had gone out sometime during the night. Physically, I felt really bad and I hadn't even put my foot on the floor yet. I started thinking, oh my God, here I go again, another diabetic day. Since I've been diagnosed with diabetes, I have days when, for no apparent reason, I don't feel well. So I try to take it in stride, knowing full well that it will pass and that more than likely something will happen during the day to take my mind completely off how I feel, both physically and emotionally. So I get busy and do what's in front of me.

My mind went to my ninety-year-old friend who is in a nursing home. I had promised him I'd take him out today and give him a little relief from the boredom of the place. It's hard for him now because he was always in the know and always with people in downtown Oceanside. He doesn't like to participate in the nursing home activities. He would much rather go for a ride and look at things he can see.

This was on my mind as I rolled out of bed and got myself ready to go to my AA meeting that I attend every morning, except for the days I'm working at our central office. Years ago, I heard a guy share that people were asking him, jokingly, what he was going to do when he retired, and he said: "Get more active in Alcoholics Anonymous." This really stuck with me, so I try to be as active as I can. After our Daily Reflections book came out a few years ago, our Friendship Center started daily morning meetings based on the daily readings. Today the Reflection read:"Frequent contact with newcomers and with others is the bright spot of our lives." I could really identify with the alcoholic who wrote realizing that we are all sort of a garden-variety human being, and the things we get the most joy out of are the things that sometimes we don't want to do. I certainly wasn't thinking about doing too much today other than taking my friend for a short ride.

I picked him up about eight o'clock and we went to the meeting, where we were greeted by a bunch of people who were very grateful they were sober. They were all glad to see him and this made my heart kind of sing, the way they treated him and welcomed him. Both of us have been sober thirty-two years now, my friend and I. Afterwards he wanted to get a haircut. One barber shop was closed and the other one had an hour's waiting time but we took that in stride.

Then we went by the senior care center where he had spent some time and he got an opportunity to talk to some of the social workers and some of the patients there and he was just glowing. I could tell he felt really good and his spirits were lifted. We left there and headed for McDonalds for a grilled chicken sandwich. I learned how to cope with his eating habits because I now have a bib for him to catch all that extra food. I used to get really upset with him when he had his nice clothes on and then he would start wearing his food while eating.

We left there and went back to the old neighborhood, in the Barrio, where we both spent a lot of time. I'm telling you this to show you how things work in our program of recovery. You just do what you know is the right thing to do. The first person we ran into was a little guy we'd met about eight years ago. This little guy has tried to sober up many times: he gets sober for about a week or two and then gets drunk again. He saw my truck pull up and started talking and thanking me for some things I had done for his son and himself. He laid it on pretty thick, so I told him I didn't have any money and not to lay it on so thick, and he got a kick out of that. As we were driving away, my friend said,"Man, you know, he sure has a good head on his shoulders and he's really educated." I said yes, but it doesn't do too much to help keep him sober, just like it doesn't do too much good to carry the Big Book on your arm all day if you don't open it up and read it.

I have been trying many times to talk to my friend about the fact that he's been blessed in so many ways, and that he's just at a place in his life where he cannot do the things he used to do and wants to do. I told him he still has a pretty good life and it's up to him to make the best of it. I try to remind him about the program and that it's one day at a time. So as we were driving away, he said to me, "You know, I really have been in pretty good health." I said, "You're correct about that. As a matter of fact, you've been in pretty good health for about ninety years. It's just that your body is getting older now and giving out on you some."

He said,"Yeah, you're right." I said:"Your biggest problem today is that you don't like where you live. We know some people today who have some very serious health problems. Think about your buddy who's been very active in the community. Now he has to cancel doctor's appointments because he can't get from point A to point B. That has never been your problem and I hope it never is your problem. It won't be as long as God keeps me involved in the Fellowship of Alcoholics Anonymous."

The last thing my friend requested this day was to go by the central office. He knew I worked there and he wanted to see the manager, who is a friend of ours. So we went into the air-conditioned office. As you walk in the door, you see the circle and triangle embossed in the linoleum. My friend saw this symbol and I asked him if he knew what it was all about. He remembered about unity, service, and recovery and the circle being the world. I felt really good about that.

I'm coming to the end of my day now and I just thought it was important to share how my diabetic day got turned around. In thirty-two years I have never, ever had doubts about whether or not this program works. I think I am about as unique as ham and eggs. Frequent contact with others and what I can do today to help others is the answer. It took a long time for me to come to this realization. I thought my problems would be solved if only. If only . . . then I'd be all right. It just doesn't work that way. It takes the little things that happened today — they're not dramatic but they prove my Higher Power works when I don't even think he's working.

I'm home now, sitting here thinking about what a great day I had, from moment to moment. It turned out that just by putting one foot in front of the other and not questioning, I was able to go with the flow. Everything was in God's hands and I really had a good day. It had nothing to do with the excitement of a girlfriend, money, property, or prestige. My friend was the bright spot in my life today, along with all the other people I came in contact with. I can honestly say that I love the old man. I love him for who he is and what he has done for me and others and tonight my heart is full. I never thought that a day like today would be a high point of my life. All that excitement that I used to crave and strive for was not there. I don't have to live on the edge anymore. And tonight as I lay my head on my pillow I can't think of one single thing that I did today that I have to go back and redo and make amends for.

Not bad at all for a seventy-two-year-old tongue-chewin' drunk.

Sam L.
Oceanside, California

Miracle In a Burger Joint

March 2002

Of all my experiences in sobriety, none can match what happened the day that the Promises started coming true in my life: it was a Sunday afternoon and I was to meet my estranged wife at a local burger joint to give my children back to her after visiting with them for a day. Our divorce was almost final, she was taking good care of our children and herself, and was moving forward with her life. Unfortunately, I was unable to accept this fact and, more often than not, was filled with fear, anger, and jealousy. These feelings were something I constantly struggled with and had to turn over to my Higher Power on a daily basis. She soon arrived, and as we were taking our food to our table, I noticed the new engagement ring she was sporting. I said, "Nice ring – where did you get that?" She looked at it, smiled and spoke his name. I could feel my blood pressure rise, and I knew that I was about to ruin the day. But instead of preparing to throw my hamburger into her face, to rant, rave, cuss, and generally cause a scene, I silently said that simple prayer that I had become so very familiar with:"God, please help me."

And that is when it happened. At that very moment, my entire world and body seemed to stop. I felt something like warm honey being poured over my mind and body. I closed my eyes and lowered my head as this warm feeling completely covered me. As I opened my eyes to look at my feet, I fully expected to be standing in a puddle of this liquid! Of course, there was nothing there, but something inexplicable had happened because when I looked back up at my ex-wife, the only thing I was capable of feeling was – are you ready for this? – love. That's right – love.

Not romantic love or any other kind of love that I've ever known or felt, but a love that I can only describe as coming straight from God. A love born of complete and total acceptance. And at that very instant, I suddenly realized that God was doing for me what I could not do for myself.

My life has not been the same since that day. And in the seven years since then, the Promises have continued to come true for me. I love sobriety and I love life. And I have my Higher Power, the Twelve Steps of Alcoholics Anonymous, and my brothers and sisters in recovery to thank for it. The Big Book says that the Promises "will always materialize if we work for them." I believe it.

Lester W.
Oceanside, California

The Ability to Love

May 1962

I have been hearing about love as manifested in our Fellowship. I heard the members talk about the privilege of making Twelfth Step calls, the love they felt for drunks. I sat through these meetings, nursing the shame that I did not always feel this.

In trying to work the honesty part of the program, I had to admit that I did not always like to call on drunks and that I had little tolerance or patience with them. I accepted the calls because I had been taught from the beginning that my sobriety depended upon it. There was also an element of fear — if I refused to take calls, I would be criticized by the group, and their approval was of utmost importance to me! When I had to call on a particularly long-bottom alcoholic, I sometimes felt actual revulsion.

This honest evaluation of my feelings was as far as I could get. I was filled with guilt and self-loathing because of my attitude. I tried discussing this with one or two other members, but they didn't seem to understand. I finally got to the point where I couldn't tolerate the word "love." Because I thought I could not experience it, I couldn't believe that others could. I called them "phonies." I cried that they were desecrating the word — practicing cheap emotionalism.

I noted that Christ had commanded us to love one another. I reasoned that if it was a commandment, then it must be a thing that could be willed. At this point I decided I must be hopeless. The more I willed it, the more elusive it became.

I have always found beauty in the Prayer of St. Francis of Assisi, have heard it referred to many times in our literature and meetings, and carried a copy of it in my wallet. One day while reading this prayer, the full realization of its meaning began to come through to me. This saintly man was praying to God that it be granted that he seek to love more than to be loved — not that he express love to its fullest, not that he express it at all, not that he seek it completely but only that he seek it more than he sought to be loved.

Hope began to grow in me. I suddenly realized that here was a man, who had lived through the same experience as I, reaching across the centuries to me. The hard core of my guilt began to disintegrate, and there came to my mind what I have always considered as two key words in AA — "willingness" and "grace." I must become willing to seek to love more than I sought to be loved and ask God's grace in granting this. We are our desires. If I began to desire the ability to love, so would it be granted.

Slowly, very slowly, I began to feel a stirring within my soul. Meetings seemed to have a greater depth. I began to feel a new emotion toward the newcomer. Twelfth Step calls were indeed a privilege. I began to feel — love? Could this be love? Yes! I remembered that there are degrees in everything! Because I had not felt the great love for mankind as expressed by a Schweitzer or a Ghandi, I thought I was incapable of any love. The old alcoholic perfectionist!

Now when I attend meetings, it no longer bothers me to hear the members speak of love. I am not sitting alone with guilt and shame. I am sharing, I belong, I am a part of the group. God grant that I may continue to seek not so much to be loved as to love.

Anonymous
Lexington, Kentucky

Miracles to Go

August 1997

I remember the best AA meeting I ever attended. It was in a western town, a noon meeting in an old building next to the railroad tracks. I was new and not talking yet. I hunkered down on the dilapidated couch, comfortable from years of use, my hat pulled low. Cigarette smoke hung from the ceiling; sunbeams streamed at an angle, landing on a very old wood floor. The coffee was strong.

The meeting began as usual, and a man was called upon to read "How It Works." He began to read very slowly: "Rarely. . .have. . .we. . .seen. . ." I thought, this is going to take forever; they should get another person to read. But they didn't. I looked at the big man slowly struggling to speak each word. His face was scarred and pockmarked. His hands were like mitts. He must have weighed close to three hundred pounds.

One agonizing word after another, and "How It Works" trickled out. The meeting was to end promptly at 1 P.M. It was 12:35, then 12:40. Everyone was silent. No one got up. Forty of us, each had our own thoughts. For the first time I'd noticed how many times the word "honesty" was mentioned in "How It Works."

At 12:45, a wave of something invisible fell over me. I knew I belonged. If there was an answer here for this man, there was going to be one for me. That hour showed me AA at its best — unconditional love and sincere hope that progress in our lives can happen.

At 12:50, the basket came around. The man was still slowly reading. Everyone had tearful eyes, including me.

Who can dispute that a miracle happened that day? This man — who, I learned later, had spent a hard life in prison — finished the last word of "How It Works" at 12:58. We all stood and held hands, and finished simply with the Lord's Prayer.

Norm M.
Cedaredge, Colorado

SECTION 6

The Joy of Living

"We are sure God wants us to be happy, joyous, and free."
Alcoholics Anonymous, p. 133

During our drinking days, we imagined not-drinking as a grim, grey, joyless affair. Where would the fun be? The excitement? But we found out that drinking was the grey world; sobriety is in full color. Sobriety offers an abundance of laughter, friendship, the excitement of spiritual and emotional discoveries, and moments of just plain joy. As we grow up and grow out of self-pity and despair, we think no picture of emotional sobriety would be complete if it didn't include the joy.

The Rhythm of Life

October 1998

In may 1993, I entered the Fellowship of Alcoholics Anonymous in the midst of a very painful divorce resulting from years of alcohol abuse on my part. My two children, aged two and three at the time, were caught in the middle of this situation. My recovery went well, and my relationship with my children continued to improve, but after seven months in AA I still felt an absence of peace. Although I'd been working on my spiritual life, I continued to find it difficult to accept the fact that my family was not coming back together. It wasn't long before I started questioning God as to his unwillingness to answer my prayers.

Immediately following my divorce, I was living in a little broken-down trailer. I was broke and I resented the fact that I no longer had a house and all the material things that told me I was okay. Even when I was an emotional and spiritual wreck, my material things had always provided a false sense of being okay. Now I had nothing, and my kids were spending their first weekend in my new home.

I tucked them into bed and went back into the living room and sat in the dark, just thinking and feeling sorry for myself. It had snowed all that day and the full moon was reflected on the freshly fallen snow, illuminating the room with its light. When I got up to go to bed, I stopped in the doorway of the kids' room. I stood there, just watching them sleep. The moonbeams shining through their window cast a beautiful haze upon the bed where they lay sleeping.

What I remember most about that night is the rhythm of their breathing. As the girls slept, I recalled the slow, steady, peaceful rhythm that I marveled at the first time I held them. The same slow, steady, peaceful rhythm was there when I rocked them to sleep in the following years. It was this rhythm that had been a constant for me in my relationship with my children. It was this rhythm that told me they were okay and that in turn my world was okay. It was this rhythm, in an old beat-up trailer in a run-down trailer park, that told me God was listening and my world was okay.

Isn't it interesting the way God whispers to us? But we don't always hear his messages. That's why it's so important for me to work on my relationship with God. I believe the divine to be incarnate in all things, but the only way I know to honor my Higher Power is to talk to him as if he were a person. I never ask him for things anymore, I don't believe he is a genie who grants wishes, but I do believe he gives me strength and hope and an appreciation of life and goodness.

This concept is of great comfort to me, and I think it's what we try to achieve through the spiritual Steps of Alcoholics Anonymous.

Frank K.
Dearborn Heights, Michigan

Hanging in There Together

March 1984

When I came on the program, in October 1956, it was in a foreign country, where there were no groups, no meeting place, no anything much. A lady passing through Venezuela on a visit carried the message and "captured" five pigeons — three men, me, and one other woman. When our traveling lady departed, she left five very dickery new members. The "oldest" was three months dry. I was last, with a few weeks, barely dry between the ears, still confused, and as nutty as a fruitcake. Our only hope was in hanging in there together, writing a lot of silly, incomprehensible questions to the AA General Service Office. We always got answers. Of course, we knew nothing of treatment centers or recovery homes. We all imagined this was how AA worked: if we wanted to stay sober, we just had to sweat it out. So we sweated and prayed and hung in there.

I'd been drinking for twenty-eight years. Though I desperately wanted what had been offered to me, I had a few slips, overnight storms that drove me insane, fearing I had lost this wonderful new life. But I really wanted sobriety with all my heart and soul. So God gave me other chances. I finally made it back to England, surrendered totally, found a group, and by the grace of God, have been sober since December 28, 1958. Miracles, miracles!

In 1961, when I got to the States and heard about recovery homes and treatment centers, I pooh-poohed the idea."They'll never make it. You have to do it the hard way; you have to suffer through your own personal crucifixion." Such arrogance! A few years later, I was joyously, happily a housemother in a home for recovering women alcoholics, 1967-69. Some of "my girls" are still sober, and I'm still their loved "auntie."

You may think I'm still nutty as a fruitcake, but I'm so happy, so overjoyed, so everything good, that I'm still on a gorgeous Cloud Nine. Now, that's really something, isn't it? Here I am, nearly seventy-eight, poor as a church mouse, housebound, and partially disabled by a couple of strokes. My floor furnace won't work; neither will my electric fire; and I'm full of the joys of spring, though it looks like snow on the Sandia Mountains. The secret is that I begin my day, every day, with "Good morning, my God. Thank you for a wonderful night's sleep."Thank God for the electric blanket!

Then, I totter out to the kitchen, plug in the coffee, feed "all creatures great and small" (five cats, once strays, now beloved companions, and two dogs, likewise strays and devoted companions). While I'm doing those chores and the coffee is perking, I look out the kitchen window. Again, I could shout my praise and gratitude to God, for sparkling blue skies (they are gray now, and it does look like snow) and for a little apricot tree, a thing of great beauty, glowing golden. Oh, thank God! There's a little story to my apricot tree. It's five or six years old, and it sprouted from a pit I spat out as I walked through the garden on the way to hang out washing. When I saw that little seed, sitting there beside the path, I thought, "Well, God bless you! Maybe if I plant you right here, you will grow." So I did, and it did, and now I have all this beauty. I even had quite a crop of apricots this year!

I am blessed, too, with endless enthusiasm for the Fellowship of AA, with its love, and with the joy of being sober and alive. At a meeting, I give my full name, say I am a recovered alcoholic, give my dry date, and tell the people,"If I can do it, anyone can do it! But you must practice the principles, follow the Steps, get a sponsor, and above all, get active."

I am delighted, when I walk into my group, to hear some of my loved ones say,"Here's old Self-Will Run Riot." Or I may be fondly greeted with "Here's our salty old bitch." I love it, they love me, and all is well. At least, it gives me a sure way of practicing my humility. It is very different from being called "that crazy, drunken bitch," as I was in the old days, isn't it? How good it is to be free of arrogance, sarcasm, lying, and cheating, to be totally honest with myself and my fellowman.

Another little gimmick that keeps me happy and sober is this: if I'm puzzled or anxious about something, I write a little letter to God and tell him all about it. Sometimes, I'm asked, "Aren't you lonely, living by yourself?" Oh, they can't possibly know the joy of solitude, when I can commune with my God as I understand him.

L. P.
Albuquerque, New Mexico

Meetings, Meetings, and More Meetings

March 1995

I have been sober for twenty-five years. In the peculiar math of Alcoholics Anonymous, twenty-five times 365 equals one. We all share the comradeship of having been sober this one day, which is the only day we really have. But as a friend reminded me a few days ago,"Yeah it's one day at a time — in a row!"

Sobriety has brought with it countless blessings, all of them in the form of people. First there is the continuing relationship with Lynn, my wife of thirty years. Thirty years married and still going. We are the avenue for each other to experience emotions that otherwise we might keep at a safe distance. I've also had the privilege of seeing my children grow up into great human beings who love me, and the birth of grandchildren who also love me.

Why do I keep coming to AA after all these years? One reason is that I laugh here more than anyplace else I go. This laughter is hard to explain, isn't it? We tell each other stories of tragedy and see in our own stories the absurdity of our actions, and we laugh together. I think it's partly relief that allows us to laugh, and partly trust — the laughter comes from knowing that someone else really understands what madness there is in alcoholism. I think also we laugh because we're glad to be alive among a crowd of others equally glad to be alive. This is laughter from heaven.

I also come to AA for the shock of self-recognition. When I hear your stories, I see myself. When I can see myself, I know that I need to be healed, restored, built up and lifted up. I come for the antidote to my own peculiar brand of arrogance, egotism, and pride. This antidote isn't a vaccine but a medicine I require in order to survive these poisons that live inside me. Meetings are where I get this medicine. And you encourage me. I am made brave — that's what "encourage" means, after all — so that I can risk little experiments at being better.

In other words, I come to learn how to be human. The Twelve Steps are a lifelong schooling in what it means to be human. Not for nothing are they called steps: in small increments of improvement that add up over the years, I learn to walk the walk of life together with you. I learn that to be human is to be a creature, that creatures have a Creator; I learn that to be human is to discover the power in powerlessness, to explore the meaning in surrender; I learn to face myself without fear, even with pleasure; I learn to hand over my failings and my successes, to be confessional and vulnerable, to live in the day, for the day's failings and successes are enough for human beings. I learn to deepen my relationship with God, and to carry the message to other alcoholics.

And I come for friendship and affection — not only the friendly and affectionate feelings of others toward me although I treasure them, but for the inspiration you give me to feel friendly and affectionate toward you. This is harder for me: to invest myself in others.

It's a characteristic of all humans, not just drunks, either to be on their way toward the best that is in them or the worst. There's no such thing as standing still. I'm either getting better or I'm getting worse. I can't content myself with indulging a little bit of badness, because it will progress. I will become a bit more bad as I age, and a bit more, and more, until by the time I'm old I will have become all of what I only indulged in at forty, but relished at fifty, and was consumed by at sixty. Allowing myself to love you, admitting to myself that I would miss you if you should die — these are ways of continuing my growth without which something much worse than death happens to me: I become that which I loathe within me. A little liar become The Liar. A little thief becomes The Thief. A little sadist becomes the Marquis. A little whiner becomes The Total Self-Pitier. You protect me from my wicked self and lift up the image of my good self for me to keep striving after. For this, I am indebted to you. For this, I love you, and I will miss you if you die.

So, in summation, this is why I continue to come to meetings: I come for sobriety.

I come to keep up my gratitude and subdue my taking-for-granted-tude. I come because this is where I laugh more than anywhere else.

I come for the shock of self-recognition. I come for the antidote to pride.

I come to learn how to be human. I come to learn how to love.

What keeps me coming to meetings after twenty-five years is certainly necessity, but necessity never did anything for me as a motivating force. It was pleasure that has always motivated me, and that is still the bottom line: I come for the pleasure of it, the pure pleasure.

Anonymous
Irasburg, Vermont

Practical Joy

February 1997

Recently, the hard work my wife and I have put in has been bearing rewards of modest material security: new house, new car, money to buy Christmas gifts and maintain a prudent reserve, and more prospects for creative work. Though we've been working for these things for several years, they've come quite suddenly in the last month. Our house plans have turned out especially well. So I enjoy telling AA friends that I spent time praying about the situation, and that what we've ended up with is not at all what I dreamed about and planned for — it's better.

People in the Fellowship have a special warmth when you share good news with them. We've all experienced so much bitterness, loss, and grief when drinking that any affirmation of life turning out well in sobriety gives our nervous systems a tingle of hope.

However, I cringe at AA meetings when I hear people claiming that their modest or great good fortune is a result of prayer:"When my car broke down I prayed for God's will to be done. And the next day my Uncle Bill called and offered me his old car for free." Over and over at meetings I hear variations on this version of how prayer works in people's lives, as though this were proof that God gives us what we need.

God is not Santa Claus, I want to shout in reply. Prayer and meditation are not application forms to some cosmic welfare program. The Promises don't say a thing about getting back any of the stuff we lost to drinking. I know because I lost everything: property, money, business — everything. In fact, my net worth in sobriety has never equaled what it was in my drinking days.

My reaction is a signpost flagging my need for an inventory, of course. The intellectual arrogance that made me a know-it-all drunk hasn't miraculously vanished in sobriety, in spite of fervent prayer to have it removed. But I still believe that, as our Third and Eleventh Steps insist, prayer and meditation are intensely practical. Just as these Steps claim, I was convinced of the effectiveness of prayer by the results I saw in my life. But this was years before I began earning back some of the material things I lost to alcoholism.

I was two years sober before I was able to recognize how prayer had been working in my life from the beginning. When I came to AA, I had no Higher Power and no clue why I needed one. What I did have was an overpowering obsession to drink that I could no longer control. My sponsor told me it would help if I prayed to have the obsession removed. So, without having any faith in what I was doing, I prayed. I also did a lot of other things my sponsor suggested. But only because I wanted the insane urge to drink to go away. My mental obsession with booze was a daily battle for almost two years.

What I could see when the obsession finally diminished was that, despite a lifetime of defiant self-sufficiency, I'd had the willingness to ask for help and then follow someone else's suggestions. This was new. I prayed daily for help with the obsession, and was given the willingness to follow directions— something I'd never had before.

I saw too that I'd been given perseverance and stamina. When this didn't yield instant results, instead of jumping track the way I had in almost everything else in my life, I continued working the Steps one day at a time. I'd always worked hard but I'd rarely stuck with any one thing very long. This was new to me too.

I began to have some genuine trust in my AA friends and sponsor. I'd never trusted anyone before, and with good reason: I thought everyone was at least as untrustworthy as me! But I was given self-acceptance. I came to see that, like everyone, I made mistakes, and that this was not reason to dislike, shun, or manipulate people. I came to rely on the fact that other people could and would help me. And I saw and trusted other people's good intentions. When I began conducting my business affairs on this basis, I saw success returning to them.

And even during the sober years when my finances were bouncing below the poverty line, I learned to be grateful for the simple life and friends and hopes that I had. After all, I'd come from a place where I had only the chaos and impending doom of active alcoholism. So I learned about the place of gratitude: the importance of recognizing that the gifts in my life were not of my own making. I did the footwork. But the results were up to God.

Beyond working the Twelve Steps, I've never understood what God's will is for me. I see that my Higher Power didn't give me the material things I thought I needed and wanted and deserved in life. My Higher Power gave me the emotional and spiritual tools I'd need to acquire these things, and also gave me the choice of where and whether or not I wanted to use these tools.

This is all in the Steps. And it's a lot more than I had when I was drinking, even though — in financial terms — I owned more then than I do now. If I hadn't been given the willingness to follow a sponsor's directions in the beginning and pray simply because he thought it was a good idea, I still would have no idea how to use the rest of the tool kit. Possibly I might have acquired the house and car and loving companion that I have today. But given the attitude I had when drinking, these gifts could have only inspired a sense of emptiness.

I still have moments like that. Well, so I have some nice things again — so what? I still feel empty and lost. What's the point? A dry drunk.

The gift today is that I have an immediate answer for that attitude. I get it every time I call an AA friend, read AA literature, talk to an AA newcomer, do AA service work, or pray. The point is to pass it on.

So now I have the means and the joy to carry the message. And what I see in retrospect is that I've had the means ever since my first sober day in AA, even when I was living on food stamps and had to borrow money during my seventh sober year. The joy was always available too. But I didn't know enough to pray for that. I had to be sober longer before I understood the practical aspect of joy. Not the joy of owning. The joy of living. To me, this is the Great Reality of Alcoholics Anonymous.

Ernest S.
York Harbor, Maine

Savoring Our Sobriety

August 1982

It was natural for us to begin our journey of happy sobriety in Alcoholics Anonymous with an anticipation of trouble in trying to live in the now, one day at a time. After all, we had spent years deeply regretting painful pasts and weeping about dismal futures.

We are fortunate that so much attention is directed during AA meetings at the importance of making life a matter of today's concern — not yesterday's nor tomorrow's. If we forget that growth is achieved one step at a time, we are doomed to flounder in confusion.

I came to AA as an agnostic. What, besides the bottle, did I have to believe in while drinking? I was started on my understanding of a Higher Power by hearing that God has time only for each today as it comes.

If God does not exist in yesterday or tomorrow, then we can be at peace with our conception of God only during the now. If we choose to retrogress into the past or project into the future, we'll be alone in our thinking, since God is not to be found in such areas. And the loneliness of stinking thinking is all too familiar to alcoholics.

Living in the present rids us of both guilt and fear. Guilt can materialize only from an errant past and fear from intrusions on unknown futures. Resentments develop only from what has already been felt and fear from apprehension about experiences yet to be confronted.

If we are to find spiritual growth and serenity, we must dress our minds each morning as carefully as we dress our bodies. Only then can today become the glorious tomorrow we looked forward to yesterday.

Because each of us, at any moment, is the sum total of every choice he or she has ever made, it is not sheer fantasy to expect each day to be the best day we have yet lived. There surely never will be a wreckage in the future as devastating as what we encountered when we were guzzlers

— so long as we stay sober.

At some point in each today, we recovering alcoholics need to pay ourselves a friendly visit. Ultimately, at our individual paces, we will get to know ourselves. Some AA members go so far as to contend that an unexamined day may hardly be worth living (to paraphrase Plato).

Today's sobriety cannot be chugalugged like alcohol. It has to be sipped, one taste at a time, so that each drop of serenity can be fully savored. It is well to remember that nothing can replace persistence as a tool for sobriety — not talent, genius, nor education.

When we alcoholics concentrate on living only one day at a time, we find that the best gift of any day is a fuller understanding of values. The things that count cease being those that can be held in the hand and become only what can be held in the heart. Hence, none of our real gifts can be stolen from us. We can lose them only through our own carelessness and complacency.

It is a tough job for most of us to avoid procrastination. Of course, procrastination does not belong in one-day-at-a-time living. We must avoid the use of the word "should." In AA growth, it is a put-off-until-tomorrow word, an indefinite word that accomplishes nothing. It invites rationalization. It is best that we substitute the word "will." "I will do . . ." rather than "I should do . . ."

Our program assures us that all answers to our daily problems are found in living in the now. Solutions that worked for yesterday's woes might be outmoded today. And reaching into the future for answers is wishful thinking.

Perhaps all of the living-today lessons we learn in AA can be boiled down into this often-made quip: a sober alcoholic who has one eye on yesterday and the other on tomorrow is likely to be cockeyed today.

C. C.
North Hollywood, California

Savoring Sobriety

August 1997

During my drinking days, my life was in free fall. I didn't think before I acted, didn't accept responsibility, didn't show up, didn't behave morally or decently. To rationalize this behavior, I presented myself to myself and others as a free spirit and a hedonist. I really thought I was a pleasure-seeker when in fact I was merely seeking gratification for my addiction to alcohol. I didn't see that my "free-spirited" behaviors — my selfishness, the carelessness of my love life, my lack of commitment, the wild unmanageability of my life — weren't choices, but came directly out of my alcoholism and my desire to evade reality. I had to see myself as a hedonist because I couldn't claim more solid accomplishments; there was in fact very little true pleasure or contentment in my life. How could there be when I didn't have any peace of mind?

Several weeks after I walked into my first AA meeting — a Monday night beginners meeting in New York City — I saw my first copy of the Grapevine. I'd already started to read the Big Book, the "Twelve and Twelve," and Living Sober. Now I was looking at the cover on that August 1982 Grapevine, and I saw this short headline: "Savoring Our Sobriety." I never thought I'd savor anything except bourbon, and here was this wonderful little magazine, which I'd never heard of before, saying,Yes, sobriety can be savored. And the Grapevine was right.

What does it mean to me to truly savor a sober life? The most important thing is that I'm in the present moment, not in the past or future; it means I don't speed by my life so fast it's just a blur; it means being quiet in my mind and not worrying about things I can't solve today or conducting conversations and arguments with people who aren't in the room. I often have to remind myself to slow down and stay in the moment. I live in Manhattan, where the preferred mode of existence is faster (cities gave us the term "rush hour," after all), and in the rush and the hurry I sometimes forget to breathe. Just last night, as I was walking down Broadway after work, I had to make myself stop to look at the evening sky and the last light fading on the tall buildings, take a deep breath from my belly, count my breaths from one to ten, and recall that life wasn't going to start sometime in the future: the moment was now to relax, breathe, look around me, be alive. Don't clench; don't grab; slow down. "Easy Does It" is very simple and very useful. Also useful is a small prayer or affirmation: please let me wear the world as a loose garment.

Something else I must do to savor sobriety is try to accept other people, even ones I disagree with or dislike, even the most long-winded sharer in my home group or the person I've heard complain a million times (haven't I tested my group's patience?). I can't savor sobriety when I'm imprisoned by "self-centered fear," so that means making a phone call to a friend, or saying hello to a newcomer, or making a point to sit next to somebody at a meeting and catch up with what's going on with them. No big deals, just simple things.

When I slow down I can take pleasure in the many good things of this world: good conversation, books, music, making a meal for a friend, taking a walk, watching a movie, having a quiet cup of tea. My husband (who is also an AA member) is an actor, and I like classical music, so we've combined our interests into an appreciation for opera and have season tickets to an opera company which is located up the street from us. Seven or eight times a year, we get dressed up and go out to dinner and then sit in orchestra seats in one of the world's great opera houses, waiting happily for the moment when the house lights dim and the starburst chandeliers rise to the ceiling and the orchestra begins the overture. What a treat! We never fail to enjoy ourselves or to appreciate the fact that we're sitting there sober; we don't take it for granted for a moment. Recently, we were enjoying a pre-opera dinner when I said to my husband,"You know, we couldn't enjoy this so much if we didn't also enjoy going out for coffee after our home group meetings." How could I enjoy the big-ticket items in my life if I didn't enjoy the little things? It's not even a matter of "big" and "little" — everything's part of a continuum. The 13th century Zen master Dogen said that a cook must prepare a simple broth of wild grasses with the same care that he prepares a rich cream soup. Savoring comes from paying attention to the task at hand, whatever it is.

I think that's where gratitude comes in: to help me to better appreciate whatever is going on in my life. Gratitude isn't a duty I have to perform, it's a tool, a form of perspective. It reminds me to appreciate the simple things: every night that I go to bed sober and not in a blackout, every morning that I wake up without a hangover.

There's a nice chapter in the story that began fifteen years ago: today I'm a member of the editorial staff here at the Grapevine. This means that for the past several years I've been part of a team that puts the magazine together and gets it into the hands of over 125,000 readers around the world. Somewhere right now, this month, a new member of AA is reading the Grapevine for the first time. And I want her to know: sobriety can be savored. This is the gift we've been given: a real life that grows more vivid and more interesting and offers more to be enjoyed and relished and delighted in. I hope that if you are a first-time reader of the Grapevine, the magazine will continue to be your companion on the journey. It's one of the ways that many of us savor our sobriety—and it always reminds me how lucky I am to have a life worth slowing down for.

Anonymous
New York, New York

The Man I've Always Wanted to Be

October 1990

In November 1977, during one of my many stays "around" the program, an Al-Anon member asked me why I wouldn't work AA's Twelve Steps. In all sincerity I told him,"I don't need the Steps to stay sober. The Fellowship of AA is enough to keep me sober." I kept slippin' and slidin' around the meetings, convinced I had this AA business all figured out.

Two months later I took what turned out to be my last drink, although I didn't know that at the time. Shortly afterward I was in a beginner's meeting, for people with less than a year of sobriety, where the topic was AA's Twelve Steps. The chairperson called on the man seated next to me, and what he said helped change my life.

This fellow was a loudmouthed, obnoxious, self-promoter who invariably took up meeting time to talk about cars, business, and anything except sobriety. He had been "around" the program for nineteen years. I despised him heartily. Imagine my surprise, then, when he puffed out his chest, folding his arms across a flabby gut, and said,"I don't need the Steps to stay sober. The Fellowship of AA is enough to keep me sober."

You might say it was a sobering experience to hear my words coming from that mouth. I looked at him and said to myself,"I don't want to be like you!" Here was a guy who'd been "around" for nineteen years, saying the same thing I'd said just two months earlier! I really did not want to be like him!

Fortunately, I had an option. A group in our town was known as a very Step-oriented, hard-core bunch with a lot of strong old-time sobriety, and that's where I went. I don't believe it was a conscious decision, but I knew those folks were different from some AA people I'd met, and I wanted to become as "different" from that loudmouthed fellow as was humanly possible. I attended the meetings for a while, and finally found a man I wanted as my sponsor. He seemed the opposite of the loudmouth, with a quiet grace and gentle manner that appealed to me. What really hooked me, though, were his frequent references to caring for a nephew who'd recently lost his mother in a car wreck. That touched me, so I worked up the nerve and asked him to sponsor me.

Never let anyone tell you that God doesn't have a sense of humor. The man I selected as sponsor was a short, rotund businessman who drove a huge Lincoln and, for some reason, hated bikers. I'm a long-time

Harley fanatic who, for some reason, hated short, fat, rich cats in fancy cars. Hence we were perfect for each other.

The first thing my sponsor told me was, "I don't have time to help you stay sick — I'm much too busy for that — but if you want to get better I'd be glad to help."

He definitely meant what he said, but my sponsor was not one of these head-crackin' types that order their pigeons about. That was just as well, because I was extremely rebellious when I sobered up, and could have seized on a domineering sponsor as an excuse to chuck it all and return to drinking. Instead, my sponsor laid out a set of tools (the Twelve Steps) and told me how he used them in his life. There were no demands made of me. He simply said, "If you want what we have, come and get it," and that's what I needed to hear.

Through my sponsor, and other members, I've learned that this program offers much more than simple dry time. They not only told me about, but actually lived, what I now know as the Promises. They explained that the Promises were an end result of working the Steps to the best of my ability, and that life in AA took on a whole new definition when compared with the miserable existence I'd known out on the streets.

My friends did not lie. I have done more, accomplished more, learned more, and gone farther in the past thirteen years than all the other years of my life put together. One of my favorite words, when I came to AA, was freedom, but my concept of freedom was limited. I thought it meant doing what I pleased, when I pleased, without regard for consequences. Now I am truly free: to walk through any given day or situation without cringing in fear, exploding in rage, getting loaded, or self-destructing; to love, laugh, and know and appreciate the simple joys that come with being alive; to be a part of, instead of apart from, a society where I can serve an invaluable purpose; to recognize and utilize my own talents and abilities, as a writer, a worker, husband, stepfather and participating member in the Fellowship of Alcoholics Anonymous. I'm free to be the man I've always wanted to be, but never before had the courage to become.

In what I see as a prime representation of AA's magic, I was offered two examples situated at opposite ends of sobriety's spectrum. Adrift between the two poles, I was blessed with a clear-cut choice, and for that I'm very grateful. I needed something just that black-and-white to penetrate the stone wall of excuses I'd built around myself. I now know, and my life in sobriety has proven to me, that I've made the right choice.

I'm also pleased to report that my sponsor has gotten over his hatred for motorcyclists, while I've mellowed somewhat in my distaste for short, fat, rich folks. As for the loudmouth? Maybe he found his own examples, because at last count he had several years of continuous sobriety, and was still going strong.

Wm. J.
Temple, Texas

A Twig In the Yard

July 2001

Bill M., sent us the following note along with a letter from his son, who is serving time in Kernersville, North Carolina

"This is a story about gratitude — gratitude in an unlikely setting. My son is halfway through a long prison sentence, the beginning of which marked a deep bottom in his life and the beginning of his recovery from alcoholism. He now serves as a peer counselor in a state-run program that struggles to make sobriety available in the prison environment. His growth and his Twelfth Step work constantly amaze me. A recent letter was so striking that I asked his permission to share it with you and your readers. It began with the news that he had finally been able to see a dentist — no small feat when it requires that he be transported a hundred miles to a prison facility that had such resources."

Dear Dad,

Yesterday at 4:00 A.M. I was awakened in order to be taken to the dentist. It was the first time in a year that I'd been outside for a ride, so I was really excited. Of course, I had to be handcuffed to a waist chain, then shackled before I could get in the van. The van was brand-new: the smell was delicious and the seat was so comfortable. I must have looked like a dog out for a drive, staring eagerly from side to side. It was amazing to be moving — and in such comfort.

When we got to the facility, they took off my chains and let me walk around the prison yard. I got to touch a tree for the first time in over three years! It was an oak tree, and the bark felt so good beneath my hand. I looked up through the branches and leaves to the sun shining through. The ground was littered with small twigs and real acorns that crunched beneath my feet. The trunk, which must have been seven or eight feet around, was covered with moss and lichens. I have never seen a more beautiful sight.

As if that were not enough, a calico cat suddenly rubbed up against my leg and gave me permission to pet him while he drank from a water dish. I was dumbstruck with all the sensation. The feel of bark and cat fur, the sight of open space and green leaves — all this for a man who'd had none of them for years — were for me what climbing Mt. Everest must be to a free man. Then it ended. We left after my visit to the dentist, yet I will always carry that day with me as a symbol of God's grace and as a reminder to have gratitude for the small, mundane things of everyday life.

A twig in the yard — what joy! I'm so glad to have you to share it with. I don't think anyone else would understand.

– Your son

Volume
II

SECTION 1

The Great Balancing Act

Though balance is one of the most underrated attributes of all, being non-dramatic and low-key, we observe that the label "unbalanced," applied to a person, is never a desired one. Balance is one of the gifts of long-term sobriety that seem to be appreciated later or, by the unusually mature, at any time.

From San José, a member describes balance to a "T" in 1976, after noting the faux ecstasies of his drinking days. "Today, by the grace of God, I strive for a basically bland diet. For example, on this day I've worked eight hours, washed my clothes, gone to a meeting, and written a poem about gratitude. Later, I'll meditate. Dull by my past standards, but pleasantly sane by my AA way of thinking."

Before he discovered Step Eleven and meditation, Ken of Ames, Iowa, writes that he was powerless over unhappiness and his life was unmanageable. "Long before I was a binge drinker," he adds, "I was a binge thinker. I tended to think incessantly." His mind had no "off" switch, coming up with grudges, resentments, and so on, creating the state of imbalance, ripe for relapse.

When Jim of Largo, Florida's home group holds a workshop on emotional sobriety, he becomes convinced that time in the program is not enough to ensure it, and that certain emotions will remain deadly because they "block me from dealing in a mature, emotionally sober way, rather than just reacting."

With his new sense of balance, Bruce H. of Arlington, Virginia, decides he doesn't have to memorize anything in the Big Book after all; neither does he have to arrange the chairs perfectly every time. And G.P. of Elbert, Colorado admits that when the pink cloud hit him, "I went insane. Quite starkly mad. ... For one thing, I couldn't say no—a clear indication of insanity. ... I accepted five full-time job offers, and was thinking of a sixth." He also bought everything in sight.

Newly sober; deeply imbalanced.

"Thank the Higher Power," he writes. "The malady doesn't seem to be permanent."

By Our Attitudes

January 1950

A little clock in a jeweler's window stopped one morning at 20 minutes past 8. School children, noticing the time, stopped to play. People on their way to the train stopped to chat a little longer and all were late because one little clock had stopped. Never had these people realized how much they had depended on that clock in the jeweler's window until the day it failed them and led them all astray.

We AAs are very much like that clock. Day after day there are those who are looking to us for guidance and direction on the way of life. If our AA life is functioning properly, we are faithful guides to all who observe us. But if something has gone wrong with our AA way of life, we are stopped clocks, and unfortunate indeed is the man who permits himself to be misled by our example. We who have been helped by AA are as letters of God addressed to our friends and fellow men. By our attitudes, our speech, and our behavior are we to show them the transforming power of AA's philosophy of life.

C.T.
St. Paul, Minnesota

The Golden Mean

(from PO Box 1980) November 1976

In my drinking days, excitement was measured by the degree of my emotions. My ecstasy came from the fleeting highs of alcohol and sex and from the appealing but dangerous depths of writings about suicide. The in-between—moderation—was despised as a malady of the "common folk."

Today, by the grace of God, I strive for a basically bland diet. For example, on this day I've worked eight hours, washed my clothes, gone to a meeting, and written a poem about gratitude. Later, I'll meditate. Dull by my past standards, but pleasantly sane by my AA way of thinking.

Bob P.
San José, California

Binge Thinker

July 2010

Before I was powerless over alcohol and my life had become unmanageable, I was powerless over unhappiness and my life had become unmanageable. I turned to alcohol in my late 40s as the best self-help option I thought I could find. Often, my unhappiness seemed to melt as I drank. But drinking became an ever more elusive and flawed solution to my unhappiness. It began to create unhappiness of its own. My overall unhappiness was eventually much greater than what I had evaded and yet not solved at the beginning of my alcoholism. Now what?

Maybe the best way to feel was to be happy. How was that possible?

Long before I was a binge drinker, I was a binge thinker. I tended to think incessantly, as if this were an essential part of staying alive. My mind either had no "off" switch, or, if it did, I had no idea where it was. In this constant banter, I could find all sorts of resentments to chew on, grudges to hold, victimization to ponder and catastrophes to protest. Life was unfair, people were the harbingers of much injustice and unkindness, and I was justifiably withholding my seal of approval by not accepting what already was.

I create thoughts. I can do so from default behaviors (what I have come to otherwise recognize as "character defects"), or I can create thoughts within the awareness of having choices. Awareness for me is realizing that I am not my thoughts. Rather, I observe my thoughts and their creation and content. If I need not be run by my conditioned default thinking, then have I discovered the choice of observing and creating constructive thinking?

Once I learned to meditate, as encouraged in Step Eleven, I was able to find the "off" switch to my thinking when that thinking is neither needed nor useful to me. I can use thought, rather than have my thinking use me. "Awareness," I believe, is the most accessible doorway to what has been referred to as "spirituality" throughout my life and in AA.

Ken T.
Ames, Iowa

It's Not the Shoelace

May 2010

Recently, my home group conducted a workshop exploring emotional sobriety. We broke it up into different aspects such as "What is emotional sobriety?", "How does it differ from physical sobriety?", etc. My assignment was to explore why we need emotional sobriety and I presented it as follows:

When I first came to AA my emotions rose to the surface, where I became aware of them. While I thought that I had successfully submerged them with alcohol when I was drinking, I can't deny that I often drank at "him," "her," "Mom," "Dad," the boss, some unfair customer, a disrespectful sales clerk, the police, the system, or whatever. I could say that alcohol let me not feel, but the truth is that I felt everything and often wanted to show "them."

I used drinking to hurt others or plot my revenge. The only blessing was that I often wouldn't even remember the plot when I sobered up. Newly sober, I not only had the feelings but I also had a lack of ability to deal with them. My immaturity came out in full force. My old idea was that alcohol would still work with these feelings, and I would sometimes give in. Even if I didn't drink, I could be miserable and hold grudges. That's when something trivial like a broken shoelace might lead me to drink because it was the last straw.

Without the help of God and a sponsor, I might never know that it wasn't the shoelace but the lingering grudge and my lack of emotional sobriety that led to drinking again. While this lack of emotional sobriety was dangerous when I was newly sober, the danger did not go away just because I've achieved some time in AA. Indeed, I can mistake number of years for a degree of emotional sobriety. I can rest on my laurels without even recognizing it.

When I hold on to resentments, when I find things unforgivable, when I am jealous of another's success, when I am unwilling to listen to others and change my mind, when I react severely to criticism even as I congratulate myself for another day or month or year of not drinking, I am not only not emotionally sober, but I also may become not physically sober. This can happen even if I once had a spiritual awakening and have many years of sobriety behind me. The Tenth Step tells me to "watch for selfishness, dishonesty, resentment, and fear" not because these emotions are so deadly in themselves, but because they block me from dealing in a mature, emotionally sober way, rather than just reacting. Since the essay on the Step next says, "and when they crop up," it is a sure bet that time in the program will not make me immune from these negative emotions and my ensuing reactions. My reactions can include drinking again, but even if I don't drink, I can cause problems and heartache in the lives of those who love me and work with me.

As the book says, "We believe a man who says sobriety is enough is unthinking." For the sake of others if not for myself, I should seek emotional sobriety.

When I am letting myself be ruled by "selfishness, dishonesty, resentment, and fear," any rational thinking or action I do would be purely by accident. Likewise, serenity would be elusive at best and non-existent at worst. As a friend says, my biggest job in a spiritual life is to become undisturbed. I would only have one of two reactions to any negative interaction with another person: I would either forgive the other person or make amends.

I have made a real advance in emotional sobriety if I finally realize I do not have to react to a slight by striking back.

Finally, I was told to live a day at a time but not told how to do that. I submit that it is impossible to do a day at a time when bedeviled by emotional chaos. If I strive for emotional sobriety, I will have a much better chance of living in the now, which can lead to joy and appreciation for the wonder of my life.

Jim H.
Largo, Florida

Carrying the Message

February 1971

After six years of sobriety, I recently went through my first really long (four weeks) depression. Doctors had given me some bad news about my eyes, and I immediately exaggerated their diagnosis. I went around telling myself I had to accept blindness and, "Thank God I would not be a drunken blind man." I thought I was applying the Eleventh Step (to the best of my ability), but I could see it was not working, and I proceeded into a very bad depression. I used all the gimmicks I was taught in AA—except "Let Go and Let God" and "One Day at a Time"—but nothing was working.

Then I met a doctor who told me things were not as bad as I thought—it seems I was hearing only what I wanted to hear. However, the depression continued. Along about this time, I had some difficulty with someone I was sponsoring, and the result was another emotional upheaval, which did not help the situation.

I began talking to good friends and members of my group, and things started to look a little better. I found my "conscious contact" through these friends. I found that "Let Go and Let God" does work and, most important of all, that "One Day at a Time" was something I had to apply. 1 also attended many meetings. I have to be honest and say I did think about drinking, but thank God I did not drink. I put myself through the meat grinder on this emotional binge—self-condemnation, doubts, etc.—but I think it was for a reason. I think I have greater understanding for someone going through these things, and I also learned to love the person who has been slipping around and coming back. Have I ever experienced such humility and willingness as that poor soul? I am feeling much better now, and I thank God for AA and my good friends. I have learned how to accept their help.

J.P.K.
Queens, New York

Chair Master

October 1997

Those first few weeks in AA, Frank had begun to drive me nuts. He couldn't resist. At the end of every meeting, as soon as I left the table and headed toward the door, he would yell across the room, "Hey, Bruce!" I would stop, turn, and wait for it. Grinning ear to ear, he would give me the wink and pointed finger and say, "Be good to yourself!" I would nod and mumble, "Sure, Frank, sure," and go to the car.

Driving, I would begin the internal dialogue: What the heck does that mean? Be good to myself? I was good to myself—that's what got me into church basements trying not to drink a day at a time, trying to understand the meaning of AA, trying to relate to guys like Frank. I'd been too good to myself—rewarding myself with booze, giving myself a break with booze, cozying into the bottle in the basement—and look where it got me. I figured I needed to do the opposite of being good to myself. I need to get tough with myself: stop this stuff that I obviously couldn't handle. How did Frank get sober and stay sober all these years, if that's his philosophy, and why the devil is he singling me out with that dopey farewell after every meeting?

But I liked Frank. There was something about him. He was a rugged, confident, good-looking guy in his forties, with a toughness about him, a directness in his approach to the AA program. He had years of sobriety and when he talked, gesturing in a relaxed way, he reminded the group frequently that his father was Italian and his father always said don't worry about it, it will always work out, and he would add, "And it all will, a day at a time, if I don't take a drink and give it a chance." When Frank talked, the others around the table smiled and nodded and gave him respect. I did too—and he seemed to like me and listened to me when I talked. Then he gave that parting shot as I was leaving!

I'm a doer. Always was. I was brought up that way. My mother told me, "You're the best; you can do anything anybody else can; set your goal; follow your star." My dad said, "Don't be lazy; get to work; I've got a job for you."

I was a doer when drinking, too. I drank through college and finished with honors (never mind the hospitalization for ulcers senior year and the medical caution about drinking). I drank through a marriage and held it together for sixteen years (it wasn't the drinking that caused the divorce, it was that incompatibility thing). I drank through three good jobs and always moved up, got promotions, made more money. (Okay, maybe the problem I had with those martinis in the last job was beginning to show a little, but I was never arrested, was I?)

Sobering up in the group with Frank and the others, I was still a doer. I ran at AA like I was running to the arms of my mother, eager to show that I was the best, ready for the compliment. I got to the church early, set up the chairs, learned (from an old guy named John) the special technique of making coffee in not one but two big pots (I'll make the best coffee, they'll taste the improvement), and on my six-month anniversary I was asked to be Friday night program chairman. Terrific, I thought, they recognize my leadership ability. I'll do the best job yet.

And I did. The Friday night programs got more interesting. I found different ways to bring everybody out, get them to speak. I passed around the "Twelve and Twelve," got people to read in turn. The group hadn't done that before. They thought it was neat. I photocopied sections of the Big Book and the Hazelden guide to get folks into the Fourth and Fifth Steps. People were responding. I felt good, proud even.

Frank kept saying, "Hey, Bruce, be good to yourself!" And I kept trying not to be annoyed. But now there was a slightly sterner tone in Frank's voice. The smile was there, but he was serious.

After I'd been sober in the group for a year, I had moved from coffee maker to chairperson to program chairperson to chairperson of the group. I didn't know that groups had chairpeople. I had been to some that didn't, but mine did and when I found out there was a leadership ladder, I was in my element. Set your goal, son. I did, in AA as out there, and here I was, at the top of this group. And I was secretly memorizing not only all the Steps but chapter five in the Big Book and key passages from the "Twelve and Twelve." I wondered if anybody had ever been able to recite, in perfect order, the names of the people whose stories were in the Big Book. That would be impressive! I resolved to do it.

Then it began to hit the fan. One Friday night an older woman named Maude couldn't read the photocopied sheet I had handed out because she had left her glasses home, and before I could show my flexibility and initiative by switching to another format or reading it for her, the next guy said, "Why don't we forget this reading stuff and just talk about it?" And before I could smile and accept this, the next guy and the one across the table were shoving their sheets into the middle of the table and growling a little. Shambles. And then John said that the woman who was making the coffee had quit showing up and what was I going to do about it. And a week after that, a small delegation, all old-timers, pulled me aside after the meeting and said (I forget the exact words, because I was so steamed): "Too much is changing. People aren't used to it. Maybe it's time for you to give somebody else a turn."

Two hours later, Frank found me. Corner table, neighborhood bar. Drinking soda. Thinking. Tired. Thinking. Lonely. Thinking. Angry. I told him, as he settled into the other chair, a little smile on his face, a nonchalant order to the waitress for "what he's having," that I was totally demoralized.

"What do you think the problem is?"

"I don't know. I was trying my best. I thought I was doing a good job, but Tom and Suzy said—"

He raised his hands. "Whoa. Tell me that part about trying your best."

"Just that. I tried damned hard to give something to the group, to make it better, if I could."

"You think that could be the problem?"

"I upset the group by really getting involved?"

"Right now I don't care about the group. I'm looking at you."

"You see a guy that's about ready to give up."

Frank took a leisurely drink of his soda and wiped the corners of his mouth with the back of his hand. He looked me in the eye and I looked away, down into the glass in front of me. But I was all ears. Frank was talking: "You know what being good to yourself means? In your case, I think it means don't try so hard. Getting sober is not some contest you have to win. You're not being good to yourself by putting yourself into a stressful situation. And AA sure is not the place for stress. It's just the opposite."

It's been more than twenty years since I left that bar with Frank, and my understanding of AA and what it means to me has grown from that moment. "Easy Does It" is not something that comes naturally to me. But within AA, it has come to make sense. Since that shaky beginning and the talk that night with Frank, I've found my place in the Fellowship. It is not up front, trying to be in charge. I try to contribute when it's my turn; I lead a meeting when asked; if chairs need setting up, I do it for fun and not as Chair Master. Relaxing in the program, in Frank's philosophy, and not trying too hard have become the gift of daily sobriety and a new way of life. Every day, every meeting, there's something more to learn. I am sober. I am being good to myself.

And occasionally I will spot him—the guy who is so uptight, the guy who is beating himself up because he's not perfect, the guy who is trying so damned hard to get it right—and I'll meet him for coffee or talk to him after the meeting. I'm not Frank; I can't say to him, in front of the group, "Be good to yourself!" But I'll tell him my story, and how I came to understand that trying too hard in AA isn't good for me. Sometimes the guy will say that it makes sense to him, too.

Bruce H.
Arlington, Virginia

Honeymoon

January 1975

Anybody who grabs the program and makes it past the end of the physical hassles—the shock when your liver finally realizes it's got a new shot at life and starts functioning normally again, when your digestive system starts to see food again, real food, and not that strange chemical that kept putting it out of whack—anybody who makes it that far enters what many repaired drunks ("recovered" sounds so medical) call the AA honeymoon. It's that wonderful period, lasting from ninety days on up, when life is so damn fine, when everything works so ... so right, somehow, that it's hard to believe you're just returning to normal and not becoming some kind of superman.

The honeymoon strikes people differently, depending on individual traits, depth of addiction, withdrawal problems, and the like. Some become ebullient, bubbling with smiles and joy; others walk around in a seemingly permanent state of euphoria or shock; still others can't believe the feeling and seem stunned. (A good friend who caught the stick the program offers told me, "Do you know, really know, what it's like to suddenly be able to tie your shoes with both eyes open?")

I went insane. Quite starkly mad. Perhaps not clinically (although everybody in the program seems to know all about psychological terms and what they really mean), but if outward actions are any indication, I was ready for the men in white coats and the quiet, screened rooms.

For one thing, I couldn't say no—a clear indication of insanity. At one point, when I'd been dry about six weeks, I had accepted five full-time job offers and was seriously considering the sixth when my wife ran screaming from the house—babbling something about my blank eyes and wide smile—to get my sponsor and save me from myself. I firmly believed I could actually do all five jobs at the same time. Worse, I accepted invitations to four parties—all on the same night. And we made all four, too, though it took my wife nine Al-Anon meetings before she mastered the twitching. She still, though I've been dry over a year now, automatically says no to everything.

On top of my inability to say no, or perhaps coupled with it, was the seemingly automatic compulsion to buy things. Anything. If I wanted it, I'd buy it, completely on impulse. I now own and will probably own forever (unless my wife sneaks things out of the house) a six-foot-high, spine-leafed Dracaena marginata, probably the ugliest plant in the world. The saleslady called it a "decorator's delight." I've since named it Igor, because I think it might be carnivorous. There are fewer flies in the house since I bought it a year ago, and we haven't seen a turtle I couldn't refuse since the day it got out of its box. To go with the plant, I got an amazing deal on a Great Dane named Caesar (who I know is carnivorous and who sleeps wherever he wants, usually on my bed). In the yard is a genuine 1951 GMC pickup that doesn't run and never will run unless I can find an engine. I bought it anyhow, at a garage sale. "Don't worry, darling," I remember saying. "Think, just think of how much money I was spending on booze. Besides, we can always use it as a planter if I can't find an engine." I also have two lamps (genuine 1934 modern chrome), a folding typing table designed by a maniac (it folds all the time), six new coffeepots (no, I don't know why), a stool made from an old milk can and a tractor seat, a case of canned smoked oysters, and an antique sausage-stuffer with—as nearly as I can figure it—eleven parts missing. There is more—you can buy a lot of stuff in three months or so. But the rest is worth mentioning only as (I wince at the word) junk you trip over.

Thank the Higher Power, the malady doesn't seem to be permanent. I have since quit buying things—unless I need them or at least think I need them. But there is apparently one lasting effect—if not on the drunk, then on the Al-Anon.

The other day, I was in a pet store, and they'd just gotten in some boa constrictors—not too big, perhaps six feet or so. At any rate, I was standing at the glass case looking at them the way you stand and look at snakes, not thinking of buying them or anything, just looking, enjoying the intricate patterns and colors, when I was interrupted by a stifled cry. I turned to see my wife standing in back of me, eyes wide in horror, the twitch definitely pronounced, while her head shook back and forth slowly. "No," she was whispering in terror, "not snakes. Please, not snakes. Anything but snakes."

And that just goes to show, it sometimes takes an Al-Anon longer to get straightened out than it does the alcoholic himself. Hell, I wasn't even thinking of buying a boa constrictor.

Not at the price they were asking.

G.P.
Elbert, Colorado

SECTION 2

THE MIRACLE OF MANAGEABILITY

"I may have a bad moment, a low hour, or a terrible day, but if I stay dry, the day will pass," says A.H. of Park Forest, Illinois. "I can't afford to get too irritated.... I've gone to sleep with a small resentment and woke up alongside an ugly giant." He then takes us through the rollicking roller coaster of his life as a pianist in a small Dixieland band, an exciting, simple life—and manageable because of our program.

The lives of active alcoholics are typically managed by alcohol, and when the relief of recovery puts the power back in our own hands, it's a sight to behold. One of the story titles in this section suggests, "Let's Take Happiness Out of the Closet." Perceptively observing that "we are not a glum lot" too often takes a back seat to sober-sided sobriety, D.C. of Bend, Oregon, is concerned that some of us feel a member is only working the program if he or she is miserable, and that some of us conjure up a negative thought just to have something to say at a meeting. "I am vowing," she says, "to give loud support to successes, not just encouraging ... troubles and failures. I now see successful living as a natural God-given by-product of successful sobriety. I say, go for it!"

"Thank God, as a result of AA and sobriety, I am liberated from dreaming the impossible dream and free, finally, to start living the possible dream," says J.W. of Islamorada, Florida, who reminds us what it was like to drink in order to transform what seemed like an ugly world.

"All the excitement and interest and wonder of adventure are mine to explore, ever-new, ever-changing, ever-becoming." Ever manageable. This is echoed by a former drama queen from Madison, Wisconsin, who still struggles with what she "might think of as having a 'mundane' life," after living only for the next big event, unaware that all of life is lived moment to moment.

Our quest for manageability never ends. Mary S.'s letter to her husband's morning group is a powerful, poignant reminder that sobriety offers us the ability to manage not only our lives, but our peaceful, sober deaths as well.

Hot Piano Man

May 1953

As long as I don't take the first drink, the door to this wonderful program remains open. I may have a bad moment, a low hour, or a terrible day, but if I stay dry, the day will pass. Another thing ... I can't afford to get too irritated. I can't choke up. I've gone to sleep with a small resentment and woken up alongside an ugly giant.

So, the prayers, the courage to change the things I can. It's possible for me to get something off my chest if it bothers me. I can talk things out. Sure, I may blow my top at times, even tell someone off. Have to come back to apologize. But don't get so full up to here that a drink is the only out. Don't shut the door.

Well, what's so important about keeping the door open? What's inside? Come on in, take a look for yourself. Meet the wife. Notice she talks freely, and seems at ease. You should see her charleston! It convulses me. But it also gives me joy. Just a bit better than four years ago an AA remarked, "She looks like she's waiting for a knight on a white charger to rescue her." Now get a load of the kids. Every one of them has somethin' goin' on, since the door is open. Saturday morning there may be ten kids in the house, but it ain't too many. I work nights but it don't disturb me. Not joy!

OK. Come on to work with me. Oh, I forgot to tell you. I'm a pianist, and have a small band. We play what is loosely termed "Dixieland" music. I like the room I work in; it's comfortable. Here, sit down anywhere and have some coffee while I do my half-hour set. The band? Yeah, one guy drinks as much and as often as he wants to, and he wants to. Another kind of watches his drinkin'. The third hardly touches the stuff, and fortunately, there's another AA in my band. So live and let live, as long as they play for keeps, and here again the program has knocked me out.

What nice guys. Honestly I can't figure it out, not if I figure my efforts alongside of my returns.

Sure I made it the hard way. No hospital; walk the streets; sweat it out; work sober in the same place I'd been drunk in before I stopped; being "not wanted" but sticking it out. Sure I admit it wasn't easy, but good gosh, who'd a thunk I'd get all this on top of escape from the rat-race?

Excuse me, coffee ain't so bad, is it? And they don't overcharge in this joint. Tell me, what is makin' good, being on top? My needs are being met, my bills get paid. Today I'm in good health, I'm playin' my rear end off. That's somethin' I never would be able to do; I'd given up on it. I chose sobriety at the cost of my ability to perform, and listen brother, no one, I mean no one, liked to get knocked out and play music more than I did. And now I'm getting' joy out of sober performance.

Yep, It's a good band, and this is living. It gets quiet inside. I don't talk much about the home within, the me inside, but you get an idea from what you've seen on the outside. "As within, so without."

Now wait a second. Don't start givin' me credit for nothin. All I did was cry like a baby. "Oh God, please help me," and then along came AA, and they told me not to take the first drink, and keep the door open. Yep, the First Step may not be the most important one; not as long as you keep takin' it.

A.H.
Park Forest, Illinois

Let's Take Happiness Out of the Closet

January 1986

"The trick in AA is to be happy and then get away with it!" A woman friend with a wry grin said that to me several years ago when I was about three years sober. I did not fully understand her odd sound of isolation or what she was saying. And how could I? I was wallowing in the pain of a lost love, barely making it financially, and confused about my job. She, on the other hand, had it made. She was married, financially secure, owned her own business, and was seven years sober.

Through the next five years of sobriety, my life gradually began to feel better and flow with more ease. At the same time, I noticed an amazing attitude in the general membership of AA toward success. Success made some people nervous, resentful, and distrustful, especially if it was someone else's!

For example, once after a morning meeting, we all met at a restaurant. I was sitting next to an amusing, laughing man. That is, he was laughing until his recovering alcoholic psychotherapist came to our table. Then he didn't feel he had the right to seek professional help and have a moment of gaiety.

Another time I saw a man of about thirty-two come into the AA club wearing a three-piece suit, beaming with purpose. He was a year sober and had finally found the direction and courage to start looking for a job. An old-timer snidely asked if he was going to get too good for us now with his fancy suit, forget where he came from, and end up drunk? Everyone around joined in the laughter (including the young man). However, I noticed the newfound confidence he had brought in with him was gone. He left a few minutes later.

I have watched and heard scenes like this over and over again in the past few years. It is as if we AAs feel a member is only working the program or doing God's will if he is miserable. I have to ask myself if AA is that way for me. How many times did I dredge up a conflict or negative feeling just so I would have something to say at a meeting? I know I often dwelled on a negative aspect of my life long enough to have a "good reason" to call a sponsor or a friend. Was I afraid I wouldn't get the strokes and attention unless I were in some kind of pain?

After eight years of sobriety, my new husband and I went on our first sober vacation. (My first ever in forty years of living!) We came back to our small home group, anxious to share our "funny" stories about "inept recovering alcoholic vacationers." We soon got the message that our comments about Hawaii met with stony disapproval. It was intimated we were bragging, even that we shouldn't make others "less fortunate" feel bad. I began to understand my friend's comment of years ago, her isolation.

I am living successfully: healthy, happy, and growing. And I think I should be after all the work I put into learning about myself and life. If life doesn't start feeling better sober than drunk, why do all the work and grow through all that pain?

I have to remember that the principle is attraction, rather than promotion. Thank God there were some sober members living successfully in my early years that I could model my goals after. Thank God YET stands for You're Eligible, Too.

I have had to fight the compulsion to validate my good life by detailed horror stories about the past, to continually prove, somehow, that I really am an alcoholic. I have sometimes felt I must apologize for my happiness.

I am now becoming suspicious of those AA folk who look down on God's gifts to others. If I can't share my successes with my fellow AAs, who do I talk to, and how isolated could I end up? I suspect that some of these people are like I was; never hoping for the good so when they don't get it, they won't be disappointed or worse yet, look the fool.

I am vowing, however, to give loud support to successes, not just encouraging pats to troubles and failures. I now see successful living as a natural God-given by-product of successful sobriety. I say, go for it!

Like my friend, I now agree: The real trick in AA is to be happy, and get away with it!

D.C.
Bend, Oregon

The Impossible Dream

November 1971

During my days as a practicing alcoholic, I had a maudlin habit that I would guess is uniquely feminine. At some point during the evening, I would weave woozily from the kitchen, fresh drink in hand, and stack a pile of mawkish ballads on the record-player. Then I would settle down to wail my off-key accompaniment. Two or three drinks later, I would be supine, a steady stream of tears coursing across my cheekbones and rolling wetly into my ears as I agonized and empathized with the heartbroken vocalist.

I am grateful for one thing: When the song "The Impossible Dream" came along, I was newly sober. Even sober, I wept over that one! And today, when I play that record, I still feel the old familiar longing for the lovely, perfect things—heroism, chivalry, nobility.

I suspect it is a siren song for many alcoholics, because most of us cherish an impossible dream. Perennially immature as long as we drink, we share with true children an unshakable faith that, if only we find the magic word, we will get the moon for Christmas. Like children, we are prone to tears and tantrums when we don't. Our tears and tantrums require special medication—and all the prescriptions contain a high percentage of alcohol.

In the motion picture *Days of the Wine and Roses,* the alcoholic wife is unable to stop drinking because, she explains, the world is so ugly when you see it sober. I had no trouble identifying with that excuse.

During the years of my sobriety, I have been one of the lucky ones who seldom think of a drink; but, if I like, I can remember what drinking did for me in the early days, the good days. I can remember the release, shyness dissolving, love welling up toward everyone, even myself. I stopped judging and criticizing; the self-defensive chip fell from my shoulder and left me weightless and free; the moon was mine at last, shining silver in my arms and worth whatever it cost!

The only trouble is that inflation sets in early in the impossible dream market. Too soon, for alcoholics, the price skyrockets; the modest hangover escalates to a day home from work, to several days home, to lost job, lost family, accidents, hospitals, jails.

"Why don't you just stop drinking?" our nonalcoholic friends ask when they see our situation. We shrug, and we smile with the charm most alcoholics can muster when necessary, and we change the subject quickly. But, in the dank miasma of the predawn sweats, when we lie sleepless and sick in the rumpled sheets, we ask ourselves the same question, and we cannot reply.

In my opinion, there is an answer—an answer we don't want to face because sobriety also has a high price tag.

We must give up the impossible dream.

For each of us, the impossible dream differs. For one, it may be great wealth; for another, a meteoric rise to fame. For me, it was a world in which love, joy, beauty, and truth (to name a few things) were the rule, not the exception. But for all of us who cherish the impossible dream, it has one common denominator: It is, as the name indicates, a totally unrealistic demand for perfection in one form or another, and it requires of its disciples a fanatical devotion that permits no compromise. We will not settle for less, and we are proud of our refusal.

We look with amused or bitter condescension at the lowly earth people who actually enjoy the mediocrity of their surroundings, their friends, their jobs, their children. Not for us, we say (going to mix another drink); at least we have the perception to spot the manifold flaws in our environment, and the sensitivity to be miserable over them. Never let it be said that we are so lacking in discrimination that we would permit ourselves to enjoy imperfection. So we stagger through the dreary drunken days in pursuit of the impossible dream, worshiping with narcissistic preoccupation our steadfast rejection of the world around us.

Listen to the words of that song the next time you hear it. If they still move you—as they sometimes do me—watch out! Unless you happen to be a nonalcoholic masochist, you are heading for trouble.

After a reasonable number of 24 hours, I have begun to realize certain truths. It is not admirable to rush in where angels fear to tread; it is stupid and self-destructive. It is not heartwarming idealism to hate life for its imperfections; it is rank ingratitude. It is not intellectual superiority to single out the shortcomings of the world; it is self-inflicted, selective blindness. Throughout my drinking years (and for the first arrogant months of my sobriety), I had a field day judging, condemning, and hating. I had to get drunk to escape being poisoned by my own venom.

Eventually, I had to free myself from the impossible dream of a perfect world in order to love and accept the real world. Judged by human standards, life is not perfect; to demand perfection of it is asking the impossible. Life is an incredible totality that ranges from good to evil, from beauty to horror, from bliss to agony. One extreme cannot exist without the other. There would be no music if high C were the only note, no art if red were the only color in the spectrum, no joy in pleasure if pleasure were the only feeling—and, paradoxically, there would be no perfection without imperfection.

What does this mean to me? Well, first it means that I don't have to be perfect. All I have to do is grow at a pace natural to me—and that is all I have a right to expect of others. If I can remember these truths, then love—real love, as opposed to drunken sentimentality—is finally within reach. It is not stupid to accept myself and others complete with our imperfections. It would be stupid not to.

It means that I am free to like and enjoy what I have. I don't need to exhibit my high values by hating my rowboat for not being a yacht, my house for not being a palace, my child for not being a prodigy. In all aspects of my actual life, there is room to grow. More important, my appreciation of what they are now has room to grow. Perfection would limit me; imperfection offers me the freedom of a million potentials. All the excitement and interest and wonder of adventure are mine to explore, ever-new, ever-changing, ever-becoming.

Thank God, as a result of AA and sobriety, I am liberated from dreaming the impossible dream and free, finally, to start living the possible dream.

J.W.
Islamorada, Florida

A Simple Miracle

May 2009 (Excerpt)

Dear Members of the Morning Meeting:

How do I possibly thank a Fellowship that helped my dear husband experience the best three years of his life? Before coming to AA, Paul had experienced a lifetime low, but in recovery he experienced a miraculous rebirth and fully embraced it. With your support he began to regenerate the wonderful people skills he had been blessed with, which I had fallen in love with 38 years ago. When he would come home and circumspectly recount how he had been able to interact with people in need, I would internally smile because I knew the Paul I had fallen in love with in 1966 was resurfacing.

Paul's last three years were his best because he had faced his issues. Freed from his hang-ups and alcohol addiction, he could once again embrace us all. When his illness robbed Paul of his ability to attend meetings, he continued his AA commitment by interacting with MGH (Mass General Hospital) personnel. Many of them responded to Paul's magic, as sick as he was, by not only talking freely to him as they were treating him, but also returning on their coffee breaks to chat. God bless him, he remained faithful to his AA commitments.

In the end, Paul was granted the grace of a happy death. His entire family—including John in Baghdad over the phone—spent the entire day telling him we loved him and sharing those final precious moments. He was able to love us all and bless us all, and he told me to tell you how much he loved you. Finally, at 7 P.M., he told us he was ready and said, "Buena sera." Those were his final words; he died 45 minutes later.

Please know, Morning Group, that Paul loved every one of you. I know he wishes that you all continue to pursue your recovery and roots for you from a higher place.

Gratefully always,

Mary S.

Life in the Express Lane

(from Dear Grapevine) May 2009

When you are in a 10-items-or-less line in a supermarket checkout, and the person in front of you has more than 10 items and that no longer bothers you, that's acceptance.

If you no longer count the numbers of items the person in front of you is buying, that's serenity.

Paul K.
Merlin, Oregon

Drama Queen

November 2010

I am one of those people who have lived under the assumption that only "big" and unusual events define one's life. One might say that I have a flair for the dramatic. Others have simply called me a "drama queen." And, truth be told, I have had a number of those unusual or profound life-changing experiences, such as growing up adjacent to one of the largest slums in the Philippines, witnessing as friends of my parents were arrested for questioning the justice of a dictatorship, hitchhiking through war-torn Guatemala the summer I graduated from college, getting married after a whirlwind romance, giving birth, getting divorced, being present at the death of my beloved grandmother, descending into the hell of addiction, and miraculously living through it to enter recovery.

These events, and others like them, did indeed help define who I am today, and I love telling stories about my adventures and the "earthmoving" realizations I came to during or immediately following them. However, the importance I have placed on having huge, unique, breathtaking encounters with life has caused me a great deal of pain. After all, life is simply not made up of one dramatic event after another, and my inability to see beyond that led to chronic depression.

In November 2002, my pain had become so great that suicide became a real option. I felt that I was, at most, a worthless shell of a human being and at the very least, rapidly going crazy. On Nov. 8, 2002, I left work to have some drinks with friends. I told my husband that I would be home soon, certainly in time to put my two young children to bed. Happy hour came and went, as did my friends, but I knew the bartender, so I decided to stay just a little longer. At 3 A.M., after closing down the first bar, giving a wary crowd a solo dance performance at the second bar, unsuccessfully flirting with one of the band members who was young enough to be my kid, trying to convince the waitress at a late-night restaurant to break the law and serve me a beer, I found my way home. This was not unusual. Nor were the hangover and the mortification of fuzzy recall the next morning. What was different was that I really "caved in" that day. I clearly remember sitting on the side of my bed, ashamed, tired, and scared, and finally saying out loud, "I think I have a problem, and I don't know what to do." To me, that was a moment of grace. That evening, I went to my first AA meeting. I have been sober ever since.

For the last two weeks, I have been racking my brain to come up with "the" profound, unusual, "wow" experience to write about for a project I am doing in school. Nowhere in the assignment does it say that it has to been a mind-blowing event. But being the drama queen, I automatically think momentous! (drum roll, bright lights, fireworks).

My mind had been spinning obsessively about the assignment, and I was becoming thoroughly frustrated. I live on the west side of town and was driving across town to get home from school last week. As I crossed the street, I noticed a particular pedestrian. She appeared to be in her 60s but she could very well have been younger. In some aspects, she blended in with the street itself, as she was dressed head to toe in worn-out, washed-out, formless grey clothing. At that moment, however, I was able to see her clearly. She was hunched over, pushing a grocery cart of junk: folded up cardboard boxes, some cloth material, plastic bags that were certainly not full of freshly purchased groceries. She was talking to no one in particular. She seemed insane.

Two seconds is not a lot of time. The two seconds it took me to cross that street had an effect on my life because I was present to see it. I don't know what the woman with the cart really is all about. I do know that many alcoholics and addicts end up on the street. That could have been me. It may even be, at some point, the fate of my own beautiful, addicted child. At that moment I was reminded to be humble, to be gracious and to feel compassion, and every recollection of that experience brings me back to that place.

I am now 47 years old. I live in a house that I own in the suburbs of a small college town. I have gone back to school with the hope of some day becoming a nurse. I regularly attend AA meetings. I have a loving and supportive partner who makes me want to be a better person. I have two teenagers who give me a run for my money but who tell me they love me every day. I still struggle with what I might think of as having a "mundane" life. But I know now that life really is anything but inconsequential.

For many, many years I lived solely for a time in the future—the next big event—or off of the tragedies or amazing accomplishments of the past. I was unaware that all of life is lived moment by moment. Being in recovery allows me to be aware and present in those moments, and every moment provides me with an opportunity for growth.

Mary P.
Madison, Wisconsin

Paying the Price for Improvement

January 1997

I am grateful to be in my twenty-first year of continuous sobriety. Looking back, it's truly amazing that I even made the first month. But my sponsor strongly suggested that I build a solid program of action based on service within the Fellowship of Alcoholics Anonymous. The actions I took in those early years helped change my life. The actions I take today enhance my sobriety and allow me to enjoy more of this great world.

Serving the Fellowship and hanging out in meetings was a good start, my sponsor said. But I must also learn to practice these AA principles in all of my other affairs. That included things like taming my temper with my family, being a better responder at work, and treating everyone with respect. Not easy tasks for a newcomer who didn't know anything about dealing appropriately with others. But one day at a time, improvements have been made.

My sponsor told me that AA would put me back into the mainstream of life and give me the opportunity to be a productive citizen. When I was 23, with almost a year of sobriety (though not completely out of the fog) it was suggested to me by my sponsor, his sponsor, and two other AAs that selling bar supplies was a great vocation for a drunk, but perhaps I should go back to college and learn to do something different in sobriety. Things seemed to click, and four years later I'd earned a college education. With this new training, and no plan of action for my life, I set out across the country in search of something.

Instead of really getting into the mainstream, however, I became more involved with general service work. Occasionally I did become involved with civic organizations, professional organizations, and church groups, but these "outside" activities were never really fulfilling, and I always returned to the comfort of activity within the Fellowship of Alcoholics Anonymous.

Doing an inventory with a sponsor on a regular basis is a valuable tool, and it was during one of these six-month inventories when it dawned on me that I'd dragged a lot of garbage with me into my sobriety. I still had a bad attitude after several years of sobriety. Yes, I'd improved tremendously over the person I was when I was drinking, but I still had low self-esteem and a negative outlook on life. I decided to get into action to improve this situation.

As my attitude began to slowly improve, I realized I'd lost my zest for life and that I had no real energy. I looked at my sedentary occupation, my eating habits, and my exercise program, and discovered I was really in bad shape physically. I started working on improving my health and have since discovered new energy along with an improvement in my mental outlook.

My professional life was the next thing that needed attention. Reviewing the different jobs and different states where I'd lived during sobriety made me realize that my resume still looked like that of a practicing alcoholic. Part of the problem was due to the fact that I'd never developed a career plan and hadn't properly prepared to become successful professionally. An AA with long-term sobriety and much service work (he was a past regional trustee) once told me that I should take the time necessary to upgrade my skills and get additional education so that I could be a good provider for my family and find a rewarding career. I remember disagreeing and saying, "AA service work is important to my sobriety." He said that I already had a program solid enough to maintain my sobriety; I'd served the Fellowship, and I could serve the Fellowship again after my professional life and family life were in order. But I still had the attitude that going back to school would cost too much and take too much time. Besides, I thought, what does this old guy know about my situation, anyway?

Today, with my changed mental attitude and improved physical health, I'm willing to pay the price to improve my professional life, and God willing, one day at a time, I'll succeed, and a better quality of life will emerge for my family and me. I now understand what my first sponsor was trying to tell me, and I know now that the old-timer was right. Man, was I slow to get this one!

The program of action that my original sponsor taught to me still works. It works for changing my life, for improving relationships, and for serving others. It works for changing my attitude, my health, and my present career situation. Another old-timer I knew used to say, "Sobriety is a constant process of uncovering, discovering, and discarding." The program doesn't wear out. If there's any area of my life that isn't right, I can apply the principles of the program of Alcoholics Anonymous and begin at once to work toward the desired results. When I'm willing to pay the price for top-shelf sobriety, "action" is still the magic word.

Paul F.
Craig, Colorado

SECTION 3

What Used to Baffle Us

It may not occur to us when we land in AA, escaping from the unbearable, that one of the precious skills we will learn is how to be comfortable with discomfort. But that's exactly what M. McF. tells us. "For the first time, I am learning how to cope with life, people, situations, not as I want them to be, but as they really are." And that results in "a living, challenging, and truly wonderful sobriety."

This theme is echoed throughout this chapter, since it illuminates one of the most promising parts of the Promises. "The world seems lost and wandering again now, but we are the lucky ones," writes G.E.H. of Cumbria in a 1975 story, even if "from the cradle to the grave there is always something wrong somewhere, something to rob us of enjoying perfection, something to bother us." Something to baffle us.

J.F. in Elmhurst, New York, writes that he never knew what to do with "a pain in my feelings," and now "when I start to get emotionally or mentally ill from indigestion of the mind, I prescribe more AA for myself. Better still, I try now to recognize the symptoms and prevent the attack." In the case of Jamie C. from West Henrietta, New York, a visit to the doctor before it becomes an emergency, actually following a sponsor's suggestions, is a brand new, sober way of doing things.

"My apologies, no matter how sincere, were not enough," says a writer about his family. "I had to find new ways of communicating with them."

That includes troublesome old Aunt Margaret, who teaches him how to forgive people even if they don't ask for forgiveness. Greg P. of San José picks up a four-year coin and remembers "that I have learned how to be a best friend to myself and that I have four years of learning how and actively trusting that part of me that was once so alien, and that I have stopped feeling ashamed of my disease and have begun to view it as a strength instead of a weakness or failing."

Also in this section we are reminded that screaming safely is one way of handling problems that used to baffle us. "Generally speaking, a good scream works any time the frustration level becomes unreasonable—say, if you stub your toe and land on your trick knee in a mud puddle while you are wearing a good suit."

Enjoy. And keep coming.

Reality Can Be Uncomfortable

July 1971

Is comfortable sobriety the new goal in AA? It would seem so from some of the things I have heard recently, during and after meetings. For instance, at a Step meeting, a young man rather proudly announced that he couldn't possibly take the Fourth and Fifth Steps because "raking up all that stuff would make me uncomfortable." Perhaps it is significant that this same young man was practically always in a state of depression and, after meetings, ran from one member to another asking, "How long does it take to find the joy and happiness in AA?"

A woman AA friend was quite upset because the local AA intergroup office phoned and asked her to make a Twelfth Step call on a very sick girl, who had just made her first appeal for help. The AA member had refused, on the basis that "being around drunks makes me feel very uncomfortable." What a tragic loss, not only for the sick girl, but for the member who walked away from an AA opportunity.

Another member, a man, has been unemployed since a short time before he came to AA, two years ago. He has specialized talent and training and undoubtedly could find a well-paying job and support his family adequately—but he hasn't looked for work because he is "uncomfortable with non-AAs." So he spends all his days at an AA club and his evenings at AA meetings. His favorite plaint to all who will listen is that his family doesn't appreciate him; he can't understand why they aren't impressed with his sobriety. How could they be? He is never at home; he keeps himself wrapped in the comfortable cocoon that is his idea of AA.

There are many examples of AAs who make similar choices in their lives, in favor of the status quo, of remaining "comfortable."

This is not for me! All my life, I have been uncomfortable in social situations, new schools, new jobs—anything unexpected. So what happened? To ease this discomfort, I drank—and finally drank myself right into alcoholism and, fortunately, AA. My sponsor told me that if I stayed away from the first drink a day at a time and followed the suggested Twelve Steps, I could lead a sober life. She didn't promise me health, wealth, happiness, love—or comfort. All she promised me was sobriety! Thank goodness, she didn't promise me anything else, because along the AA path I have found sickness, death, unhappiness, and considerable discomfort. But I have also found the greatest joy, love, and happiness of my life.

For the first time, I am learning how to cope with life, people, and situations, not as I want them to be, but as they really are. Many times, this means accepting a challenge and perhaps being uncomfortable. But it also means accepting life, rather than hiding in AA in order to evade people or situations.

If your goal is "comfortable sobriety"—enjoy it. As for me, I want to continue growing up to new experiences and a living, challenging, and truly wonderful sobriety

M.McF.
Millburn, New Jersey

The Great Art of Living

(from PO Box 1980) June 1975

The world seems lost and wandering again now, but we are the lucky ones; we have the AA program to help us rise above it, and in spite of it.

If we hope that things will one day work out perfectly, we are mistaken. Does that depress you? It needn't, for the fact is, from the cradle to the grave there is always something wrong somewhere, something to rob us of enjoying perfection, something to bother us. When we put one thing right, another will surely go wrong sooner or later. So it behooves us to enjoy every minute we can, for a minute lost is a minute gone forever.

The happiest folk are not the folk without a care in the world; they are the folk who have a genius for happiness, and enjoy themselves even though quite a few things are wrong. The great art of living is to make the best of things as they are.

G.E.H.
Cumbria

Got a Pain in Your Feelings?

March 1950

I've been in AA, and sober, for five years. But I still bruise easily—at times. Just when I think God is in heaven and the goose hangs high, something is said or done and—ouch!—I've got a pain in my feelings again!

Ever have that happen to you, a pain in your feelings, just when you had begun to pride yourself on your forbearance and humility? If so, you and I are brothers under our alcoholic skins.

What causes it is immaterial. Whether my grievance is real or imaginary, is of no consequence. Whether I'm right or wrong, I haven't the kind of temperament that can handle a resentment.

It has been my observation that a pain in our feelings can easily become, and often does, the pain of an alcoholic hangover and remorse. Most of us have a low boiling point. It doesn't take much, unless we're careful, to get up a full head of steam in short order. Leave it to us to dramatize or accentuate something out of all proportion to its actuality or significance.

Something derogatory, perhaps, is said about us. We suffer from an unjust accusation. The sincerity of our motives is questioned. Someone doubts our ability to stay sober even in AA. An individual refuses to forgive us or to try to understand our efforts at rehabilitation. We get a bad break at home or on the job. Or a person is unkind or maliciously mean. Our animosity is aroused. We put ourselves on the defensive. A resentment or bitterness is stirred up that can upset our emotional balance.

A pain in our feelings (and that's all it is, really) is preventable if we pause to remember in time just one thing—namely, that a man or a woman, and specifically the alcoholic, is his or her own worst enemy.

If someone were to take the food out of our children's mouths, get us dispossessed from our homes for non-payment of rent, inflict alcoholic convulsions or D.T.s on us, have us thrown into jails or hospitals, or otherwise mistreat us inhumanely, we would look upon him as a monster.

If he were to blacken our reputation, destroy our personal integrity, cheapen our self-respect or make us lie, cheat, two-time, or double-cross, we would be right in looking upon him as monstrously evil and diabolical, with destructive powers.

Has anyone ever done all or many of those things to you or me? No! But we've done them to ourselves while the craving for alcohol was upon us. No one has ever harmed us the way we've harmed ourselves, our families, and our friends.

Let's think of that the next time we begin to get a pain in our feelings about injustices, the criticisms of others, or the realities of life.

Why should I, for example, be resentful against truths, gossip, or malice of others when I was my own worst enemy in the past? When I hurt myself and my family far beyond the power of any friend, relative, or stranger to do likewise?

Personally, I look upon a pain in my feelings as temporary indigestion of the mind. When I get a stomachache, it is generally because I've eaten something that hasn't agreed with me. Likewise, my mental indigestion comes from some story, bit of gossip, or circumstance that I've swallowed without thinking.

When I'm in physical pain, I get relief by medication. When I start to get emotionally or mentally ill from indigestion of the mind, I prescribe more AA for myself. Better still, I try now to recognize the symptoms and prevent the attack.

The next time you feel hurt, outraged, bitter, or resentful—the beginning of many a slip as attested to by AA speakers—try to remember quickly that you haven't been mortally harmed.

In nearly all cases, it's just a pain in your feelings!

J.F.
Elmhurst, New York

Step Ten: Up Close and Personal

October 2007

I don't like going to doctors. But this sponsor of mine has a rule: if it bleeds, swells, or hurts for more than twenty-four hours, call a doctor.

So, "Call your doctor," was his suggestion when, one day, I casually mentioned a dull pain around my right ear, an annoyance more than anything, although at times it throbbed a bit. And no, I didn't know why it was hurting, though I thought it might have had something to do with swimming a couple days earlier and, yes, it had been going on for a few days.

I've heard that some people do what their sponsors suggest at breakneck speed, but I'm not in that group. A week went by, and my sponsor said, "How's the pain? Have you called your doctor yet?" I answered the questions in order: "Still as it was, but not getting any worse" and, "No; I tried, but his phone was busy." Silence from him. Then: "Don't you think you need to do a little more work on your Tenth Step?"

Tenth Step? What did the Tenth Step have to do with it? Personal inventory ... when wrong ... admitted it. What did this have to do with an earache? "Just read the Step," he suggested. "You've heard the words at every meeting. But maybe you need to understand more of what they mean." So I did what was suggested. Not at breakneck speed, of course, but I did it.

"Continued to take personal inventory": "Continued" was easy enough, since it refers to an ongoing process I do frequently—sometimes daily or even minute-by-minute. "Inventory" was also easy. It was an echo of the Fourth Step, where I did an inventory of myself.

But then I noticed a difference. It was always there, so how did I miss it? In the Fourth Step, the inventory was "moral"; in the Tenth Step, it is "personal." Was the different wording significant?

Perhaps it was; perhaps more than I'd first noticed. Bill W. warned us against complacency or self-congratulation ("After Twenty-Five Years," Grapevine, March 1960) and reminded us that, unless we keep growing, we fall back. It seems to me that one of the major purposes of the last three Steps is to keep us from complacency, to keep us growing so that we don't fall back into our old, sick ways and perhaps even into active alcoholism. Of course, that growth needs to continue on the moral level and we need to "inventory" it. But my inventory, and growth, also need to include all that I am as a "person," and that includes my spiritual, mental, emotional, and physical dimensions, to say nothing of how I relate to other people. And so, taking a "personal" inventory means that I attend to all aspects of myself, of my "person," including, but not only, the "moral" part of me.

"And when we were wrong, promptly admitted it." Over the years, how often had I heard that line and misunderstood it? At first, I thought that it meant to pay attention only to my faults or character defects. But that's not what the Step says; and, in fact, in the "Twelve and Twelve," Bill W. writes that we need to be aware not only of our limitations, defects, and shortcomings, but also of our strengths, talents, and successes. In short, we need to take a balanced approach to ourselves. Should my "personal inventory" reveal that I am off-balance in any aspect of myself, I should "promptly admit it."

"Admit it": This is not a mere acknowledgment that something about my person is off-balance, that some aspect of me needs correcting, but, once that's done, I must take action on restoring the balance. From first to last, AA is a program of action. It is not particularly useful for me simply to admit that some aspect of myself needs correcting and then to do nothing about it. Admission that something is the matter is the doorway to growth; but there will be no growth unless I follow up the admission with action.

My meditation on the Tenth Step showed me some powerful ways of applying it to my life that I had not seen before. Since alcoholism is an illness that affects all aspects of me, recovery from alcoholism must then include all aspects of me. For me, working the Tenth Step properly means being attentive to my moral growth—as well as my spiritual life, my mental and physical health, my emotional well-being, and my relationships with others. Should I find anything "wrong" about any of these aspects of me, I need to correct it as soon as I can.

"How's the pain now?" my sponsor asked some weeks later. "Gone," I replied. "Ear infection. Good antibiotics. Good doctor." And, I thought, Great Tenth Step!

Jamie C.
West Henrietta, New York

Four Years

December 2010

Monday night I got my chip. It is a four-year chip and it signifies simply that it has been four years since my life changed, four years as a survivor of a suicide attempt that was the end result of an active disease known as alcoholism.

I first viewed alcohol as a friend, a nice aid to help me with the emotional roller-coaster of the end of a relationship. It also served to help me sleep during that time. I had had the mistaken belief, because of an afternoon school special on TV years before, that it took at least four years of heavy drinking to make an alcoholic. To my view, I had only been doing that for about five months, so I still had a good three years to go before I needed to start cutting back.

What eventually happened was that I became despondent and drank to excess nightly. One day after getting off work, I drank, blacked out, and thought it would be a good time to just end it all with a massive overdose. I came to four days later in the hospital.

At first I was convinced that my problem was simply an inability to keep from harming myself. I was suicidal and I needed help for that. I was suicidal because of my breakup five months before.

However, the only treatment my HMO offered was group therapy every day, in a chemical dependency recovery unit as an outpatient. At that point, with my close brush with death, I figured I needed any kind of therapy that I could get. I didn't really care if it was for people who ate too many snacks and tried to shoot presidents, I needed anything that would not allow me to be alone with myself. I could no longer trust who I was because I had tried to die.

I had always been afraid of death. I was terrified of it and it was inconceivable to me that I would try to bring about my own end. But the group therapy in this type of group, after four days, made me realize that the attempt had happened after a bout of heavy drinking and in a blackout, and that was not normal. On Christmas day 2004 I realized that I was, clinically, an alcoholic.

I was devastated. I had always had my own opinion of what an alcoholic was. It obviously was someone who was weak-willed and immoral. But that could not have been further from the truth.

For an alcoholic, no amount of "will" can keep one from drinking again and again when the disease has reached a certain stage. It is an obsession of the mind and a craving of the body. The only hope is to beat it into remission and that requires very hard and intensive work.

Now I see that my alcoholism was an inability to handle life in an ordinary way, which resulted in an inability to keep from harming myself.

So when I picked up that four-year chip on Monday, it moved me. It reminded me that I had added four years of full living to my life that had come pretty close to extinction. It reminded me that I have learned how to be a best friend to myself and that I have four years of learning how and actively trusting that part of me that was once so alien, and that I have stopped feeling ashamed of my disease and have begun to view it as a strength instead of a weakness or failing.

How? Because for me, it means that I have learned to face some of my own dark monsters and have accepted them to the point that I can move past them. That I have developed a pattern of relating to my world that actually works, without harming myself or others in the process, and that I have learned to do so without the aid of alcohol. I am not my disease; I just have it. I have learned how to live and I have started doing so.

Greg P.
San José, California

Scream!

April 1975

Once the initial step is made (old Step One), and you're over the hump and on the way to recovery, and after the honeymoon—when damn near nothing can bother you—you suddenly find yourself in a strange world, where it's necessary to cope with the problems of life in a completely new way: You have to do it without booze.

Different people, naturally, use different methods. Some old-timers get an incredible, beatific smile and—using a secret method I haven't found yet—turn the whole mess over to their Higher Power, whose shoulders are strong enough for anything. Others make a meeting, or two meetings, or fifty—depending on the size of their problems. Many grab a phone and pick up the power of somebody else who has had to handle a problem without booze. All good methods—but for some members, they just don't quite get it done.

I, for instance, scream. This was not my first choice. Indeed, for the going-on-two years that I've been sober, I've experimented widely, with an intensity surpassed only by the intensity I used to drink with. I had some initial success with curling into a fetal position and sucking my thumb, but it caused my wife embarrassment when I did it at a party. She tried to pretend she didn't know me and, when that didn't seem to work, explained to all the people that I was a writer and that every time I got a new idea for a novel, I acted this way.

So I scream. It was either that or start going places alone, and everybody knows how bad it is for an alcoholic to be alone. I would like to expound on the many benefits of screaming as a means of fast relief from problems. It's handy, doesn't cost much, and takes virtually no time at all to bring into effect—unlike getting to a meeting or trying to phone a fellow AA whose line is busy. If you're thinking of trying it, however, a few helpful hints might ease the way.

First, don't hold it down. Really scream. Otherwise, the desired effect usually isn't achieved. A muffled urk or squeal serves only to make the frustration deeper. Reach down into your guts and pull out a bellow that rips the air, thunders around your head, and makes every hair on people's necks jump to attention. If you're going to scream, scream right.

Now, here is a secondary point on the screaming remedy: when to use it. I've found that the big problems tend to take care of themselves, or that old HP steps in before they get out of hand. No, big problems don't require a scream. It's the little nasties that can grind you down.

A classic example is what I now term The Morning of the Runny Eggs. While I was dressing, the back pocket ripped loose from my new pants when I put my billfold in. I broke a shoelace while tying my shoes. I sat down to breakfast, and my wife had goofed and left the eggs runny. At that moment, I could feel it building. Runny eggs make me ill. But I ate them anyway—the way you do, pushing the runny stuff away with a corner of toast—and had things held almost in control until I walked outside and saw a brand-new tire on the left rear of my car flat. On the bottom. On the same list where runny eggs are number one, tires flat on the bottom come in a damn close two, and it was too much for me to take.

Feeling the frustration building to a danger level, I threw back my head, closed my eyes, opened my mouth, and let out pretty close to a record-breaker of a scream. My throat was sore for two days; my wife said the window above the kitchen sink actually rattled; and—miracle of miracles—my frustration vanished. Unfortunately, my small, sweet border collie, who has big brown eyes and is gentle and was the only one who used to love me when I was drinking, happened to be following me, the way she usually did, when I cut loose. To put it mildly, she wasn't ready. Most of her hair will grow back in time, but I don't think she'll ever again follow me out to the car, or anywhere else.

That incident brings up the final point on using screams for immediate relief of problems. Placement of the scream can be all important. If you get stopped for a traffic violation, for instance (and isn't it wonderful that you can't be nailed for drunk driving?), it is most decidedly not wise to let a scream roar out while the policeman is writing out the ticket. He might break his ballpoint. And everybody knows how those boys hate breaking their ballpoints. Wait until he's given you the ticket and gone down the road, around a bend; then open up and let go. You might scare the hell out of a truck driver or a tourist driving by, but that's a lot better than making a cop break his ballpoint pen.

The only other thing about screaming is knowing when it will or will not feel right. Generally speaking, a good scream works any time the frustration level becomes unreasonable—say, if you stub your toe and land on your trick knee in a mud puddle while you are wearing a good suit.

Or if you're doing a short piece for the Grapevine and it starts to get out of hand and gets longer and longer, when you know they only want short pieces, and you suddenly realize with mounting panic that you have absolutely no way of ending it and that it could just go on and on maybe forever, a whole, epic, thousand-page work on screaming while your family starves and you just keep sitting there writing away about .... Aaaaarrrrggghhh!

G.P.
Elbert, Colorado

The Fire Has Gone Out

September 1997

I didn't have to be told that in the years of my drinking I damaged those closest to me. My wife's tears and the pain on my children's faces as I erupted again and again in alcoholic rage played a large part in bringing me to crisis and then into recovery. I knew I needed to make amends to them. I wanted to put my involvement with my family on a healthy, functioning, and mutually rewarding basis. There was work to be done, and lots of it.

The Big Book turned out to be right: My wife and children were generous in accepting my apologies, eager to help me heal, happy that the long nightmare in which we all had lived was now over. But that was only the beginning of the process of making amends to them. My apologies, no matter how sincere, were not enough. I'd damaged my loved ones and deprived them of the kind of husband and father they had a right to expect; now I needed to grow out of self-centeredness and selfishness, and to learn to look at the world from their point of view in order to understand what I might do for them. I had to find new ways of communicating with them. All of this took time, to say nothing of that rare quality, patience! It wasn't by accident, I realized, that we undertake the Ninth Step only after we ourselves have become strong enough to embark on the kind of spiritual work that amends-making requires. Perhaps we can expect the Promises to come true only after we've started making amends within the family.

As difficult as this process sometimes was in relation to my wife and children, it took on a new dimension when I turned to making amends within my family of origin. In my own immediate family, the major damages were done by me, and I was the one who needed forgiveness. But there had been no knights in shining armor in my family of origin. My alcoholic father damaged my codependent mother and she damaged him; frightened and angry as I was, I damaged both of them and they damaged me. Aunts and uncles and cousins and grandparents—mutual damages seemed to be everywhere. Everyone was a player, and in all honesty—perhaps because I'd left home in my mid-teens—my contribution to those damages had been relatively small.

But I still needed to clean my side of the street, and I saw that I had to begin by forgiving those who had hurt me. With smoldering resentments still eating at me, I couldn't be really effective in making amends. I hadn't expected it, but forgiving others for the injury they had done to me was a necessary part of my Ninth Step.

But what would it mean for me to forgive those relatives of mine who had made my childhood so unhappy? Clearly it was more than merely mouthing the words, "I forgive you." But what more? And how was it to be done? The Big Book, so helpful in many other matters, didn't really give me the direction I needed. Neither did the "Twelve and Twelve." In a small handful of places, both sources mentioned the necessity of forgiveness—of asking forgiveness of God and of other people, for example, and of forgiving others as well as oneself. In two places, the Big Book even implied that we should forgive and forget. Forget? Forget being beaten? Forget being sexually molested? Forget being neglected? Forget being publicly ridiculed and shamed? These childhood experiences were burned into my memory. Even if I could forgive those who had harmed me in these ways—and the Big Book, unfortunately, didn't tell me how to do that—I didn't think forgetting would be possible.

It turned out, however, that after eleven years in AA, I learned something about forgiving someone, and also what forgiveness means. I learned this lesson by finding myself in a kind of do-or-die situation in which forgiving turned out to be the only good option available.

My mother had died suddenly and I had to return to my original home for her funeral. In the confusion of the next few days, one idea kept nagging at me: I would have to meet, I would have to be involved with, my father's sister, Aunt Margaret. Aunt Margaret! During my childhood, although she was sometimes kind to me (but there weren't many of those times), she was more often unkind, missing no opportunity to criticize me cruelly, even to the point of publicly embarrassing me. Negative in her attitude toward me, bullying, judgmental, insensitive, at times malicious—all of these came with Aunt Margaret. In my mind she'd become a living symbol of much of what my unhappy childhood involved. To have to deal with her—and I could no more avoid doing that than I could avoid going to my mother's funeral—was to raise the ghosts of an unhappy past.

Frankly, I didn't have the emotional or spiritual "energy" to handle Aunt Margaret on top of my own confused and conflicted feelings over my mother's death. "I don't know how I can do this," I said to my sponsor. "I don't know how I can handle the funeral, that whole crazy and sick family of mine, and Aunt Margaret at the same time!"

"Can you try to change the way you see her?" he asked. "Can you see her not as the tormentor of your childhood, but as a pathetic human being who has always wanted something she never got in your grandparents' alcoholic household—simply to be loved for herself? Can you reach around your own pain and touch her hurting spirit? Can you show love to her?"

"But I don't love her," I replied.

"I didn't ask you to love her," he said. "I'm suggesting that you act lovingly toward her, or at least try." I remember thinking: I can try—but it won't work.

I had no sooner arrived at my family's house, where I stayed during the funeral period, when the door opened and there was Aunt Margaret, an odd half-smile on her face. Here it is, I thought. This is it. God, give me some help with this. I went to her. "How kind of you to come," I said. "Thank you for doing this for me. It is very good of you." I hugged her close. (I didn't lie. Everything I said was true.) Aunt Margaret began to cry and I did too. She loved my mother and she was grieving. The old dragon was then just an old lady, perhaps frightened that her own death might not be very far away. Some time later that evening, as she was leaving, I said to her, "I'm going to the funeral home tomorrow to make final arrangements. I'd really appreciate it if you'd come with me to help me through it." She readily agreed (was she surprised I had asked her?), and that established what was to be the pattern of my involvement with her over the next few days. I took opportunities to invite Aunt Margaret to be with me, whatever it was I was doing. I was signaling that I wanted to have her by my side. I was behaving lovingly.

Since then, seven years ago, there have been changes, significant ones, I think, in our relationship. I call Aunt Margaret on Mother's Day and at Christmas and on her birthday. When her husband died suddenly, I called frequently. She writes me and I write back. No, she's still not my favorite person and it hasn't happened that I've come to like her, much less develop a warm, intimate relationship with her. Perhaps it never will. Perhaps, too, it would be different if I were living near to her rather than across thousands of miles, and had to relate to her frequently and face-to-face. That might severely test my resolve to keep acting lovingly toward her! But the reality is that while memories of the past flicker from time to time, the pain of those memories is no longer there. The fire has gone out.

In all of this, Aunt Margaret never once asked for my forgiveness. Probably she doesn't know that she needs any forgiveness from me. So I've learned the surprising truth that I can forgive people even if they don't ask for my forgiveness, even if they don't realize that they need it. Forgiveness seems to depend more on the love of the one who does the forgiving than on the lovableness of the one being forgiven.

One last learning. I discovered that there is a meaning of remembering that goes beyond its minimal sense of just being able to recall. To remember in this sense means to refuse to let go—to keep something from the past alive, to give it weight in the here-and-now. In that sense, I no longer remember the pain Aunt Margaret caused me. I've forgotten it.

Jamie C.
West Henrietta, New York

Gimme Shelter

March 2010

After living rurally for six years with my two daughters, it became necessary for me to move back to Christchurch, New Zealand. I had eight weeks to prepare for moving and I looked at many homes. They far exceeded what I could afford. My past behavior, when looking for property, was to rent what I wanted and get the nicest home, despite the burden it would cause the family financially. This time my thoughts had changed. I could not afford to rent anything that I had viewed so far. Doing so would take the food from our bellies, clothing from our backs, and heat from our bodies during the bitter winter months: My thoughtless actions would cripple the family.

I put the problem in my Higher Power's hands and I put my name down on a government listing for a home. My need wasn't considered urgent and I could be waiting at least a year before a place became available. "Keep us informed," said the housing officer, "of any changes to your circumstances." I kept up my search for a property.

Several incidents occurred. My estranged husband, actively alcoholic and suicidal, went missing; my car's gearbox failed; and my oldest daughter was in a car accident. She had missed payments on her insurance. Also, my elderly mother fell. As I kept notifying the housing officer of the changes in my affairs, I felt his looks of disbelief.

One morning I awoke and crumbled inside. I just couldn't face another day. I called out to God in tears, "I cannot do this anymore. It's too big for me. Please, I give it all to you!" I did my daily readings and my prayer and meditation. I felt a peace and comfort within me that was hard to explain.

I continued doing what was in front of me. The police found my husband safe in his mother's home, after a four-day bender. We rented a car and I sold my car, getting a very good price for it. My daughter's car went in for repair and negotiations began with the insurance company. I still had not found a home, and the day arrived to move. At the last minute, I found affordable accommodations for us: a tent site just around the road from my mother. We were going to stay in my four-person tent and experience a new adventure. The park had all the amenities that we required, plus the bonus of a playground and a swimming pool. Our belongings went into storage. The move into the tent changed our situation on the housing list—we rose into the urgent register because a tent wasn't permanent housing.

We'd been living comfortably in the tent for six days when my mother died. Prior to my recovery from alcoholism, she and I could not be in the same room for more than five minutes without fighting. But with 14 years' sobriety, I could be with her and do for her what I should have done for so many years.

Over the weekend, I did what was needed with my family and returned each night to the tent with my girls. Several people had offered to house us, but I turned them down. The moments since my mother died were the closest I'd had with the girls. I wanted to stay just where we were. We cried, we laughed, and we shared stories about my mother, their grandmother. It was a beautiful time together in the tent.

When I rang the housing officer to tell him that my mother had died, he said he would do all he could for me. Half an hour later, he called: We had a home. It was too small, but I was going to take what was provided. Then he called back: Another home was available, this time with exactly the requirements I had requested from the agency. Without hesitation, I said, "I'll take it."

I know today that because I kept walking the road of recovery with joy and love, accepting and giving thanks, we were provided for.

I am still in this lovely home. I have landscaped the property with a backyard garden and an area of fruit trees and spring bulbs in remembrance of my mother. With this experience, I truly made the decision to turn my will and my life over to the care of God, and then I got out of the way.

Jennifer P.
Christchurch, New Zealand

SECTION 4

More Will Be Revealed

Recovery doesn't happen overnight, and neither does addiction, but we do get some gifts quickly. "After about five months," says one member, "the sensations of genuine feelings began to emerge. I honestly didn't know what these waves were that were washing over me, and feared I was going insane. ... Then, one sunshiny day, I learned how to smile. ... Today I can look upon myself and others with understanding, acceptance, forgiveness, and love. ... Recovery is a wonderland."

"I didn't know I suffered from terminal restlessness," writes another. "I knew nothing about true happiness, not even that I didn't know." He then beautifully describes how he goes after the desired state of emotional sobriety: "[I am] trying to locate myself at the center of the universe, searching for just the right intersection of job, relationship, friends, possessions—a magic geometry of people, places, and things that would let me love myself. ... Sober emotional stamina and patience give me a sense of continuity that I never knew existed when I was drinking and new to AA."

"Life to me is a combination of greatness, ecstasy, awfulness, painful awareness, bewildering blindness, and, at times, awesome clarity," says another, noting that it takes a mature sobriety to deal with it.

Emotional immaturity is by no means a new phenomenon. From a 1940 letter: "In our alcoholic days greedy materialism, hate, self-sufficiency, bitter resentments, and egotism, underscored with alcohol, seemingly compromise the sum total of our self." Then we learned to make "proper distinctions" and "We could not help but feel a genuine elation of the human spirit in being unselfishly kind to someone."

That might be a description of the "quiet place in bright sunshine" that Bill W. writes about in "The Next Frontier."

These uncomfortable states of mind are not restricted to newcomers or active drinkers. It might be a surprise to learn how much sober time this writer has: "*As Bill Sees It* showed me just how full of pride—the negative, not the positive kind—I was; also, the selfishness, the self-centeredness, the superiority complex to cover up the inferiority complex—that puffed-up feeling of being the most important person in the whole wide world."

This member has nineteen years, but because she never left the rooms, she knew where to turn to set herself right: "The night when I finished reading the story "Freedom from Bondage" in the Big Book was so beautiful. I identified completely with this woman, and a sense of peace, serenity, and well-being came over me. ... I know now exactly where I lost myself."

Change to Spare

February 2007

When I was still drinking, longtime friends would sometimes ask what I was up to, and I'd answer that I was in transition. I was a musician and a carpenter who couldn't find enough work, so I bounced from job to job.

"It's never boring," I assured anyone who asked. "And everything changes, right?"

Vain about my detachment from career, financial security, or any real focus, I touted what I thought was freedom—that is, until I heard a sober alkie speak about it at a meeting. Until then, I didn't know I suffered from terminal restlessness. "Self-will run riot" is never boring. Neither are fear and chaos and skirmishing through life. I knew nothing about true happiness, not even that I didn't know.

When I got sober and started working the AA program, old drinking friends offered condolences and chemical substitutes while I cleaned up my act. "Don't wanna change too radically, do you?" someone asked. My family wanted to know, "What is he into this time, and how long will this fixation last?"

The loss of a small business, a ten-year marriage, and all my property and money kept me bound to a steady paycheck during my first few years of sobriety. I had a sponsor and a weekly home group, but I also traveled, visited, and test-marketed many other meetings. I was also single, so I kept an open door to relationships.

There was always the next new thing to try, a new page to turn, a new chapter to start, or something else just down the road that would be better than what I had. It would be different this time, too, and it would give me that satisfied feeling that I remembered from the few times when booze got my brain chemistry just right. Drinking taught me that getting to the next level required burning some bridges. So, for years I prepared myself to drop everything, walk away, and start over when the next new thing called.

I didn't see myself trying to locate myself at the center of the universe, searching for just the right intersection of job, relationship, friends, possessions—a magic geometry of people, places, and things that would let me love myself. Given sobriety, a patient sponsor, the willingness to work the Twelve Steps, and eventually some professional help, I slowly came to understand.

Now, I've come to believe.

After twenty years of drinking and eighteen years sober—twelve of those investing time, money, and talent in work that I love, but work that has yet to yield a balanced livelihood—I'm on the threshold of yet another major change: a two-year graduate program that will open a path to a well-established career. This new direction is not something the fly-by-night, under-employed, stoned musician would have been willing to think about, much less act on.

Working the AA program has given me the faith that opportunity, understanding, and growth are inherent to mistakes and misfortune. And success is more a state of heart and mind than a sum total of material assets. I've learned that the best things in life aren't things, so today I pray for my Higher Power's will to be done, and for the power to carry that out.

I'm not burning any bridges this time, either. I'm not leaving behind any baggage, unfinished business, or unfulfilled promises. This change has grown slowly from my sober encounters with risk and adversity. My decision comes after years of prayer and meditation and long talks with other sober alcoholics. This time I'm bringing everything I've learned and most of the people, places, and things that I cherish along with me.

I'm not uprooting myself, turning a corner, or shooting off in a different direction. Rather, I am following an outgrowth and extension of the central fact of my life. Sober emotional stamina and patience give me a sense of continuity that I never knew existed when I was drinking and new to AA. I understand now why Bill W., in *Twelve Steps and Twelve Traditions,* considered prayer, meditation, and self-searching to be "intensely practical" and "would no more do without [them] than we would refuse air, food, or sunshine."

With this great set of tools to bring to a new career, this change isn't a magic bullet or a departure. It isn't the solution to all my problems, and it isn't going to fix me.

But man, is it ever gonna be fun!

Anonymous

Recovery is a Wonderland

July 2010

One Sunday in 1983, a major turning point occurred in my life when I walked into a convenience store. They were selling a certain brand of beer I liked for the first time in Florida, so I bought a couple of six packs to celebrate. Why do I remember that occasion so well? Once I started drinking that day, I was not able to stop. It was as if I had crossed an invisible line that had always been there; my descent into the abyss began. The abyss was the dark void of pain, shame, fear, and loneliness that had always existed within me. Drinking alcohol somehow made everything bearable, it anesthetized my feelings and let me forget my fears.

Soon I was in complete seclusion, isolating in my apartment. By then, drinking had become my entire life. I lived to drink and drank to live. Alcohol became my lover, best friend, and confidant. Nothing else mattered, except having another drink in my hand.

At times I would try to stop. Professional therapy, rehab, antabuse, controlled drinking, sheer willpower, substituting drugs for drinking, hospitalizations—nothing worked. I had become a prisoner of my own making.

On Saturday, July 23, 1988, I started drinking at noon. By six that night I was in a blackout. I woke up on Tuesday morning with a doctor leaning over me in the intensive care unit of a local hospital. The doctor said I had taken all my pain pills and was very lucky to be alive.

We talked. For the first time, I opened up to another human being. I surrendered. He listened as I described my feelings of guilt, shame, and remorse about my drinking and using. I poured out my life story: losing both my parents as a young girl, being separated from my biological family, getting adopted against my wishes into a different culture, enduring every form of abuse, going through the death of my son, and numerous life-threatening situations including surviving cancer. Now there was this: the incomprehensible demoralization of alcoholism.

Then the doctor gave me the gift of hope. Twelve-step meetings were brought into the hospital once a week and the doctor suggested that I attend. I went to my first meeting, where I picked up a white chip to signify my desire to quit drinking and start a new way of life. The next week I went back and heard complete strangers telling my story. This is where I belong, I thought; I'm in the right place. Two weeks later, I left the hospital. I continued to go to meetings every night, got a sponsor and began to work the Twelve Steps of Alcoholics Anonymous.

In the process of recovery, I gained insight into myself and the diseases of alcoholism, addiction, and relationships. After about five months, the sensations of genuine feelings began to emerge. I honestly didn't know what these waves were that were washing over me and feared I was going insane.

Then one sunshiny day, I learned how to smile. In the program I've learned that I am not responsible for anyone's happiness except my own. Most importantly, I learned that true happiness is an inside job—this was major growth.

July 24, 2010, will be the 22nd anniversary of my new way of life. The story of my recovery is a story of redemption and rebirth. It's the story of two lives in one.

Today I have become the person I always wanted to be. Today I can look upon myself and others with understanding, acceptance, forgiveness, and love. I have discovered the true meaning of the word joy. The Promises have come true. Recovery is a wonderland.

I attribute my continued sobriety to a blessed state of grace contingent on my spiritual condition. The dictionary's definition of the word grace is "unmerited divine intervention and love." During my most difficult moments, I would often contemplate the words from the old Southern spiritual "Amazing Grace" and somehow that inspiring hymnal always gave me the hope I needed. I have spent years looking everywhere, trying everything to fill the void that existed within me. Nothing worked, until the day when I started working the Twelve Steps and began looking within.

Eve Marie
Brooklyn, New York

Stuck in a Funk

December 2010

After 22 years of sobriety, I started slacking on my meetings, from two to three per week to one meeting per week (my home group meeting). The calls to my sponsor became a little less frequent as well. I started feeling disconnected from Alcoholics Anonymous and all the gifts given to me—God, fellowship, Steps and sponsor—all of which equal sobriety for me.

Aside from the position I hold as intergroup rep for my home group, my service was nil. I got to meetings as they were starting and stopped hanging out for the meeting after the meeting. I stuck around, just not for long, and surely not nearly as long as I had while practicing my "regular" program. I now know this led up to the funk I was to feel as a result.

This totally negative space I was in occurred due to changes in my life while living "life on life's terms" instead of seeking God's directions.

I had learned through Alcoholics Anonymous to accept many of life's changes as positive turns in my recovery, and to grow through them rather than look at the negatives. And so I had to take the action.

I was reminded that if I thoroughly work my program with no half-measures, if some negative thinking did occur, it wouldn't go too far, and I would be able to transition back into positive thinking more smoothly. As usual when in that space, I could not pinpoint the reason for it. I told myself there was no need to analyze: "This too shall pass."

I did not want to drink, but I started to notice that I was handling situations differently—not very well, to say the least. As a result of my lack of willingness to continue working the program that had worked for me, my patience was growing very thin, I was worrying about financial insecurity and I was isolating more and more. Situations that used to baffle me were baffling me once again and I was not handling these situations as I once had when working my program and attending regular meetings. I came to realize, coming out of the negativity, that it would never have progressed as far as it did if I had continued to do what I was doing for my sobriety, because it had been working.

Thank God I was still in a semi-sane state and made the decision to reconnect before it got to the point where I allowed my disease to shut out my awareness. So let me tell you about a few of the "God coincidences" since I made the decision to reconnect.

I went to the monthly intergroup meeting, only because of the commitment I had as intergroup rep for my home group. First—thank you, God—had I not made that prior commitment, I could see myself easily going from one meeting a week to none in my less-than-willing state of mind.

At that meeting, they asked for volunteers to distribute 50 gratitude cans to groups that had not yet picked them up. I immediately snickered to myself, while looking up, knowing that my God was behind that request.

With God on my shoulder giving me a loving nudge, and knowing it would help me to reconnect, I volunteered to take eight gratitude cans to meetings in the Coral Springs area, where I reside. Keep in mind that while I was graciously accepting this volunteer work, my head was telling me, Well, it doesn't mean you have to stay for the meetings; you can just deliver the cans and leave before the meeting starts. Well, don't you know that each time I brought a can to a meeting, I stayed for the meeting. Again I was thinking, I don't have to stay for the whole meeting; I can leave early. Once again, not only did I stay for the whole meeting, I stayed for the "meeting after the meeting" as well. (All except for one meeting; I didn't stay for a men's meeting.) As a result, I made seven meetings I would not have gone to, left to my own devices.

During this time, I went to my home group. On my way to the meeting room, there was a woman standing outside, crying while holding on to her 16-year-old son, telling him she wasn't sure she could go in; she was scared. I asked what she was scared of.

She said she wasn't sure she should be there. I told her son I'd take care of her, that she'd be OK, and he left on his bicycle after telling her he'd be back. I told her it was a friendly group on the other side of the door, and that it was a beginners' meeting. She said, "That's me." I said, "Sounds like a God coincidence to me."

I told her I'd show her where the coffee and pastries were, and I got a couple of seats for us. Then I got a meeting schedule and passed it around to the women for their names and phone numbers for her.

The format of my home group is speaker/discussion. After the speaker, the chairman asked if anyone with zero to three months would like to share. I encouraged her to raise her hand, tell everyone her name and let them know it was her first meeting. She stood up and did just that, and when she sat back down we held each other while she cried.

Just before it was time for chips, I was explaining the chip system to her. She immediately started responding with reasons not to take a chip. "I think I'll wait, go home tonight, think about it, make sure this is something I can do ...." People turned to her, encouraging her.

She made that long walk to pick up the white chip. When she returned to her seat, we once again held each other while she cried. She was feeling happy that she picked up that white chip! She kept saying thank you as she held the chip up while looking to the sky.

She stayed for the "meeting after the meeting," and her son sat with us. At that time, she shared that she had been to a meeting once before with her son and had a bad experience—someone told her that she hadn't hit her low point yet. Because of that she had no desire to return and hadn't gone to any more AA meetings ... till my home group meeting. She told her son she loved the meeting and everyone there. I let her know that there are over 800 meetings in Broward County, so if she ever has another experience like that, she has many other options for meetings. I also let her son know about Alateen.

As I was saying goodnight to her, she held up her white chip and said, "Laura, this is all because of you." I cut her off and responded with, "This is all because your God chose me as an instrument for you."

Six days have passed. I'm not sure if she attended another meeting since then; I have not heard from her again. She had my phone number.

Needless to say, I am hoping to see her at my home group meeting again. And if I do, I will be getting her phone number for Twelfth Step work to stay connected. Funny thing is, she was so appreciative of me for helping her, but I am even more appreciative of the gift I had that night in helping her—she helped me so much more!

Talk about God working in my life yet again at a time when I'm reconnecting, huh? This is an awesome reminder to me that my God is awesome; that it isn't all about me, it's about helping the newcomer; and that I am so very blessed to be in a position to be able to help others.

Laura S.
Coral Springs, Florida

Carrying the Message – Life!

June 1966

I had difficulty agreeing with the article, "Mental Depression," in the March Grapevine. Doesn't mean that I am right. Just means that my experience and understanding are of a different texture. To me life is far too complex to feel that there is a single answer even with the use of the AA philosophy, as much as I love it all.

Life to me is a combination of greatness, ecstasy, awfulness, painful awareness, bewildering blindness, and, at times, awesome clarity. The whole thing is too gloriously wonderful and awful to seek simple and lasting answers. Temporary answers, yes, but not lasting ones. The temporary answers that come through working the AA program are, to me, breathers until the next dark and glorious episode. Though I struggle, and at times hate it, I would have it no other way.

E.M.M.
San Francisco, California

Mail Call for AAs at Home and Abroad

March 1949

In our alcoholic days greedy materialism, hate, self-sufficiency, bitter resentments, and egotism, underscored with alcohol, seemingly compromised the sum total of our self. We had only a vague notion of the Higher Power.

After we had a spiritual experience through the medium of AA we were brought into closer contact with the Power greater than ourselves. After we had a clear notion of his true significance, he dissipated all our false ideas concerning ourselves and our relation to the universe. He immediately became our tutor and our guardian and revealed great truths to us which changed our materialistic and alcoholic thinking.

We were taught a new philosophy of life. We learned to make proper distinctions and grasp the true meaning of spiritual, moral, and social values, all of which were obscure and meaningless before. For the first time in many years we enjoyed a good book and knew what we were reading about. We recognized the sorry plight of another alcoholic or perhaps a non-alcoholic and rushed to his aid.

We could not help but feel a genuine elation of the human spirit in being unselfishly kind to someone. We found that true morality has its inevitable compensations, for when we benefit someone we increase our own happiness.

God Didn't Follow Orders

July 1984

Two years ago, all hell seemed to break loose in my personal life. At that time, I was approaching my nineteenth year of sobriety, and my life was definitely unmanageable—eighteen years or no eighteen years.

My sponsor and the old-timers had warned me about complacency a long time before. I had to make a commitment to myself.

In the following seven months, I read *As Bill Sees It,* the "Twelve and Twelve," and the Big Book. I honestly couldn't remember the last time I had read any one of those books.

As Bill Sees It showed me just how full of pride—the negative, not the positive kind—I was; also, the selfishness, the self-centeredness, the superiority complex to cover up the inferiority complex—that puffed-up feeling of being the most important person in the whole wide world.

An old-timer in the group I used to belong to would call me Queenie, and he wasn't kidding, either. It used to annoy me no end and even make me mad sometimes! He was merely saying, "Queenie, you're only another little fish in a big pond." But by then, the barriers were so thick and so high he couldn't get through.

As Bill Sees It merely touched the tip of the iceberg. Now it was time to get into the "Twelve and Twelve."

I read the chapters on two Steps each night before going to bed. It was all brand-spankin'-new to me. In my early days of sobriety, I had read the "Twelve and Twelve," but it had an entirely different meaning to me then. This time, different questions were being asked, and different answers were being sought.

Each night after reading, it seemed to me as if part of a veil or curtain was being lifted just a little. The night after reading Steps Seven and Eight, I cried. Step Eight especially had supplied most of the answers. What a tremendous relief! This Step talks about a person's being either on top of the heap or on the bottom of the heap. That was me, all right. The last page of the chapter talks about ending our "isolation from our fellows and from God." That's when I cried.

No specific time nor even a specific year of sobriety can be given when my terrible, terrible feeling of isolation from my fellow human beings and from God began. But it did. The phone hardly ever rang anymore; no one wanted to pick me up for meetings anymore—I had to call a cab to go to one meeting a week. The list could go on and on.

And boy, was I ever mad at God! I was telling him in no uncertain terms exactly what he should do in my life, and he wasn't doing it. The job that was being prayed for so hard didn't come. The aunt who was so seriously ill with a lung disease wasn't healed; she died.

I couldn't go on like that indefinitely.

The night I finished reading Step Twelve, it seemed as if the veils or curtains were all lifted at the same time. I realized I had become exactly what my sponsor and the old-timers had warned me against—a complacent old-timer.

Now, it was time for my next commitment: to read the Big Book. I read two chapters each night, and the Big Book was all brand-spankin'-new to me.

Every night, there would come at least one insight, sometimes more. When I read the prayer regarding total and complete surrender of my life and will, the relief was just that—total and complete. My morning prayers and meditation took on a whole new dimension.

One morning when I was saying my prayers, I thought: Am I ever lucky that God didn't get mad at me when I was praying specifically and giving him orders about my life! He knows, really knows, that I am a human being, and he truly loves me—good and bad. In addition to saying the prayer of surrender in the Third Step every morning, I sincerely admitted that there wasn't one single, solitary character defect or shortcoming that I wanted to hang on to anymore. I started saying the recommended prayer to have my character defects removed. The beautiful results of praying and seeking God's will in my life are far from passive.

Neat things, really neat, started to happen.

My isolation from my God just evaporated.

The telephone started to ring again; I was amazed when I got three calls in one afternoon. One was from a lady I sponsored four years ago. She is still sober, and we had the nicest visit. Before she hung up, she said, "I love you," and I said, "I love you, too." A friend of mine always says, in Bill's words, "AA is 'the language of the heart.'"

Then there were the visits from long-absent friends. After meetings is always the nicest time, when everyone is relaxed, honest, and open. One friend came by one afternoon unexpectedly. When I opened the door, she said, "You look terrible without your makeup!" I wear makeup at meetings, but not at home.

Through a series of phone calls, I was put in touch with acquaintances who were just waiting to become friends. They started to pick me up for meetings—places I've never been to before—several times a week. Each week, it varies.

My isolation from my fellow human beings has also evaporated.

The night when I finished reading the story "Freedom from Bondage" in the Big Book was so beautiful. I identified completely with this woman, and a sense of peace, serenity, and well-being came over me. It was as if I had been pressing a different key each night on a computer, and all of a sudden all of the insights came on the screen. I know now exactly where I lost myself. I know now exactly where my written inventory will begin.

In fact, when I'm all finished writing it, I would like to imagine the old-timer who used to call me Queenie sitting on a white, fluffy cloud in AA heaven with a twinkle in his blue eyes, showing his wry sense of humor, and saying something like: "Well, finally! Nobody has to call her that any longer."

V.P.
Toledo, Ohio

Powerful Simplicity

March 1984

An old-timer challenged me once: "Can you tell me what love is, in one word?" I thought and thought, and finally gave up. "Energy," he said. I'd been watching this man closely for a long time. The nearer he gets to the down-and-outer in the meeting room, the more he sparks up. He's our group's "unofficial janitor"—always there, serving in a thousand ways. He sponsors new ones and old ones, spent years in H&I (hospital and institution service), and is now active in public information. The other day, he spoke to a sizable group of staff psychiatrists at a local hospital; they stayed over to keep listening to him, gladly missing their lunch hour. They must have been wondering: How can such complexities in human beings be turned into such powerful simplicity?

By love. This old-timer has come to know what it means to be a trusted servant. He's around. There's something in him. A group in our city recently placed these words in our newsletter: "Help! We need old-timers at our meetings." He responded. But he is only one. It was a good reminder for me that all of us, old and new, need one another in gut-level, often desperate, intense ways. Of AA's co-founders, Bill W. and Dr. Bob, the Big Book says: "Both saw that they must keep spiritually active." And the sentence that follows describes spiritual action: "One day they called up the head nurse of a local hospital. They explained their need ...."

Together. Where can living energy go if it can't find its home between the older and the newer AAs? Sometimes, I've seen that old-timer enter a meeting depressed, for the weight of humanness is no less his than ours. And during the meeting I've watched discomfort lift from his face, to be replaced by a gentle, knowing grin.

Somehow, the inner energy that is love connects all the parts of us—our emotional, mental, physical, and spiritual selves. The first law of physics finds that energy cannot be created or destroyed. It's already all here; it can only be transformed into other energy—"new" energy, always moving, always mysteriously, on its own paths. This energy, or love, permeates the air and our inner lives when we're together; the more we drink it in, the deeper our insights become and the more "moments of perception" we're likely to have, wherein the "roots of reality ... will hold fast despite the high winds of the forces which would destroy us, or which we would use to destroy ourselves." (*As Bill Sees It*).

Another natural law reveals that the whole is equal to more than the sum of its parts. In an appendix of *AA Comes of Age,* when "A Friend Looks at Alcoholics Anonymous," the following line stands out: "For in AA the whole is truly greater than the sum of all its parts. The infusing power of the group, of our Fellowship, draws something more out of each of us than any of us by himself can supply." That certain "something more" must be understood by each of us in our own way, yet it also needs to be passed between us.

I am eternally grateful to old-timers who hang around and challenge me with impossible questions that lead ultimately to the possible quest.

Anonymous
California

SECTION 5

Rooms of Our Own

Back in the 1940s, articles in the Grapevine expressed alarm at the possibility of "old-timers" getting stagnant, even though AA itself was barely in its adolescence. One member, sober for 14 years, writes, "But here I was, sober, healthy, loved, solvent (if barely), but temporarily defeated by monotony, insignificance, and discontent. God had not signed on to my tacit bargain that I'd be a better servant in exchange for a bigger bank account."

Our disease, cunning, baffling, powerful, sneaks up on us, plays three-card monte with us, springs at us from nowhere. "Meetings in the Bank" is a terrifying tale of a member about to undergo surgery and the danger he faced. No, this time it wasn't pain pills putting him in danger. It was a nameless despair, a desperate pessimism, and it took his impressive bankroll of past meetings to prevent him from succumbing to it. It wasn't clear what the voice of despair wanted him to do. But he didn't listen, went ahead with the surgery, and writes:

"After almost four years of limping through life, I walk the Road of Happy Destiny free, light, and out of pain. The walk of a sober man, who recovered from surgery quickly in the middle of the long, slow recovery others have always wished upon him." He wasn't at a meeting, it was too late at night to call anyone, but his long, slow recovery, based solidly in past meetings, came to his rescue.

Consider the Old-Timers

June 1949, By the Editor

Consider AA old-timers—those fellows who've been continuously dry and happy for four, five, six, or more years. Everybody takes them for granted. They have no problems! Or have they? The Number One problem, drinking, has receded almost to the vanishing point. Economically they're pretty well straightened out. Some, in fact, are already working on their second millions. The family snarl, if any, has usually been desnarled either in a reunited brood, a new marriage, or a comfortable retreat to single blessedness.

So what's the problem?

It's not easy to describe. But it's nonetheless a real problem. Some say it's a restlessness, an unsatisfied feeling, an unwilling boredom. It's not mutiny nor is it any criticism of AA. It has come out of nowhere to attack men and women whose faith and good works in AA are beyond all doubt.

All of us have had spells like that but have usually snapped out of them as we came out of a more or less routine depression. Even those oddities of nature, nonalcoholics, have such lows. But a great many AAs have had "it" move right in, perched like a ghoul of gloom on their shoulders, poking its nose into all their affairs. "Hmmmmm! Not having any fun, not getting much lift, eh chum?"

There's little danger of them taking a drink. They're not hysterical. But they are concerned. They blame themselves and keep their vague fears and doubts to themselves. Then, little by little, they begin to find out that others feel the same way—usually along about the fourth or fifth year. Some get it earlier, some later. Some, apparently, never get it.

Frank discussion, getting it out in the open just as they did with their original alcoholic problem, has helped many to understand what has happened. In the early days and years when things are happening with almost breathless rapidity we get a terrific sense of growing. We can feel our personalities change. Progress, real and tangible, can be measured almost by the day. After a while that slows down a bit and we start to take charge of ourselves emotionally. We realize we are becoming adults, at long last.

By this time we've usually done a good share of Twelfth Step work, we've spoken at more meetings than we can count, we've served as group secretaries, on committees, and generally run the gamut of AA activities. Then, consciously or unconsciously, we retire, stand down to let the newcomers take over—an AA Tradition. Then it is, apparently, that we enter into a period of stagnation. We all understand that we don't dare stand still. If we're not growing, we slip back. And any alcoholic should fear that—and fight it.

So what to do? The old old-timers, those WBBB boys (With Bill Before the Book), probably had the same troubles. But they worked them out individually and not much was said or heard about it.

Today, however, AA has reached a point in years and in numbers where there are (estimated) between 10,000 and 15,000 of us who've been dry successfully for four years or longer. What percentage are feeling disquieted and looking for new worlds to conquer there is, of course, no way of knowing. But from a sizable sample it would seem there are enough to make it something to consider on a movement-wide basis.

These people want to do something about it, get together in meetings and apply the old group therapy again, only this time not to the direct problems of alcohol. They don't want to sing any psalms or beat any breasts or preach any sermons. But many feel an urge to dig a little deeper into spiritual matters. So they're going ahead, realizing that they are departing from the AA script somewhat.

No one remembers better than these self same AAs why we don't go too deeply into the spiritual phase of the AA program in our own regular meetings. Because they know that the newcomer, frightened, God-shy and skittish, can easily be scared off. We're all pretty much convinced that, whatever our understanding of God, he smiles his approval on our method of letting each new drunk find his own way.

Yet these old-timers have a new thirst and want to get on with it. Some have done it in small groups, quietly. Others have sought and found help outside AA in their churches. Now another and larger group on Long Island have begun regular meetings, patterned somewhat after the regular AA meetings, but stressing the spiritual.

Some AAs are going to point out that AA is not a cult! They're going to say, and maybe they're right, that if you're looking for God you'll never see him more completely at work than at any AA meeting.

That, in fact, may be what these experimental meetings will prove. If so, fine! These restless old-timers are not attempting to set up an "Advanced AA" with themselves as preceptors. These meetings are open to all, whether dry ten years or ten minutes. These experimenters are willing to face the prospect of utter failure, which itself may teach. After all, AA itself was founded on trial and error.

The AA Grapevine ventures no opinion. We're merely reporting. Whatever comes of this particular project, success or failure, is of minor consequence. The main thing is, that if there's a problem, whether it be a mere growing pain or a genuine ache, that problem is now out in the open.

Easy Does It—Live and Let Live—and by the grace of God, it too will get solved.

Continuance

October 1998

I don't have time for this right now, I thought. But I pushed myself away from my desk and said, "I can't offer any advice that you haven't heard before, James. When it comes to living sober, I've learned that being original doesn't work." These were words that my sponsor had once shared with me.

I was too backed up with work to take time out for this. As I'd told my wife, I was too busy losing money to be there for others. But I also wanted James, my sponsee, to feel better about the problems that filled him with guilt and despair. I felt desperate myself, listening to how much he wanted relief, and knowing I was powerless to change things for him.

Besides, I was wrestling with a few old character defects of my own. Creative work that I'd devoted months to had received unanimous rejection. Washing over me were waves of what, as an active drunk, I used to call depression; I know it better now as hurt pride, envy, resentment, and self-pity.

"It's simple, James," I said. "Stop expecting everything to turn out the way that you demand. In the long term, Steps Four through Nine provide the best plan I've found for taking care of the kind of problem that's bothering you. And to be honest, that's all I understand about how things work. If you want to feel better right away, ask God to help you to be of service. Get to a meeting. Reach out to a newcomer. That's what works for me."

"Yeah, I know," James said impatiently. "I'm going. Tonight, probably."

"Probably, James?" I said. "There's no 'probably' about the disease you and I have. Untreated, it definitely, not probably, destroys us. But my sponsor promised me that I would know a new freedom. My feelings of uselessness and self-pity would disappear. He didn't say 'probably.' He promised. But there are conditions. I have to thoroughly follow the path others have followed." James knew I wasn't doing well financially. I'd been told ten years before that probably I'd have some success in my field. Probably.

These are not the expectations that had propelled my recovery fourteen years before. Self-acceptance, life on life's terms, powerlessness, being right-sized, God's will for me: At the beginning, these were code words for me hitting my stride at last, rising—albeit slowly and with hard work—on my golden dreams of money, power, and prestige. After all, only someone with as much genuine humility as me could properly rededicate such rewards to bringing God's will into being.

But here I was, sober, healthy, loved, solvent (if barely), but temporarily defeated by monotony, insignificance, and discontent. God had not signed on to my tacit bargain that I'd be a better servant in exchange for a bigger bank account. And I was powerless to uplift a new sponsee whose problems seemed to me a simple matter of taking inventory and making amends.

"Hey, I've got an idea," I said. "How about you and I go to a meeting right now? The nooner starts in forty-five minutes. You can go tonight, too."

James had three quick excuses to beg off, none of them convincing.

"There's always something, isn't there, James?" I said.

"What?" he sounded defensive. "You think I'm making this stuff up?"

"No," I said. "I think your disease is. Mine still does. I've just learned to listen to other people's guidance a little better. That's the only difference between you and me—I've had more practice listening to other people's advice. So I've got a frame of reference bigger than the noise in my head."

James rang off with a firmer pledge to make the evening meeting. But he still sounded angry with me.

Which, when I had a moment to think, deepened my own funk. Look at you, sober fourteen years, and you can't sell your work, can't pay your bills, don't have any prudent reserve, and you can't even help another drunk very well either.

That noon meeting was suddenly looking pretty good—even if I was too busy losing money. I hopped in my truck and headed into town. The speaker opened his story with words his sponsor had given him that day: "The best way for me to succeed and grow in sobriety is to follow the advice I hear myself giving others. This is how sponsoring others helps me most."

During the break a friend who works in the same field as I do listened to my complaints about lack of success. He said that he approached doing the work the same way he did sobriety. Regardless of circumstances, you just keep doing it, one day at a time. "Continuance," he called it. "And it helps too to drop out of the debating society. Nobody promised we'd get to understand more about how the universe works than anybody else. Just a little more than we did as miserable drunks."

Yes, I used to be miserable—and lying, thieving, cynical, violent, suicidal. That certainly cast light on my present problems.

Returning to work that afternoon, I already knew I'd be going to the meeting that night as well. Whether or not James made it wasn't important. I needed to. Following my own advice worked better than thinking my way out of my problems. I planned to stick with it for that day. I had the time now.

Anonymous
York Harbor, Maine

Not on Fire

March 2010

A few days after I came into AA I was at a meeting and the topic was gratitude. With just a couple of days sobriety I was still full of anger, resentment, shame, guilt, and fear. The world had failed to give me what I felt it owed me and everyone in it had let me down. Life was painful and hopeless. I absolutely did not feel grateful for anything!

When it came my turn to share I said, "My name is Regan, and I have nothing to be grateful for, so I'll just pass." The long-timer next to me leaned over and whispered in my ear, "Be grateful you're not on fire." What the heck did that mean?! I turned and glared at him with the meanest look I could muster, but he just smiled at me. That old man and his comment made me even more angry. I still continued going to meetings, listening, and trying to figure out what people were talking about. It took a few weeks, but eventually I began to understand what that man had been trying to tell me.

I had been focused on all the "bad" things in my life. I was pretty much homeless and had been sleeping in cockroach-infested abandoned buildings and even a dumpster before coming back to AA. I was unemployable, I had no money, and I had lots of legal and financial problems, some of which I was looking at jail time for. I had abandoned my son, destroyed my marriage, and my father had told me that if I ever came near the family again they would call the police. There was nobody who understood how I felt or who even wanted to be around me, let alone help me! Now here I was, living in some halfway house in a town I didn't even like, and sitting in this stupid AA meeting with all these losers! How could anyone be grateful for any of that?

But gradually, I began to see that good things had started happening in my life. True, I still had strained relationships and the same legal and financial problems. But I was sober!

I had a roof over my head and a warm bed to sleep in. I had food to eat and clothes to wear. I was surrounded by people who really understood me and were willing to help me, expecting nothing in return. This is what that old man was saying to me. No matter what is going on in my life, no matter how bad things seem, I can always find something to be grateful for if I just look hard enough.

Even now, many years later, I can still occasionally put myself in a place that seems utterly hopeless with seemingly unbearable circumstances that I am certain I cannot possibly survive.

Then I remember what that old man said and I know there has to be something to be grateful for if I am only willing to change my attitude and look for it.

I might have to start with just being grateful I am not on fire, but once I get that, I can always build from there.

Regan G.
Mesa, Arizona

AA for Two

December 1960

On August 23, 1959, I found myself in a real jam. Not that I hadn't been in a jam most of my life, but this was different. The night before my wife and I had erupted into conflict. It was basic; it was family; it was financial. Thinking it over this next morning I felt inwardly sickened. Here I was, with five years of sobriety, hopeless and powerless. I loved my wife dearly. This breach was frightening and intolerable.

I picked up the Big Book. My eye fell on a passage I had previously marked. It had to do with the taking of Step Three—surrender. It said, "We found it very desirable to take this spiritual Step with an understanding person, such as our wife, best friend, or spiritual adviser."

I deliberated. We were spending the summer in a remote New England countryside. I had no best friend. Then it struck me suddenly that there was a minister, not of my faith, in a nearby village. I had met him once or twice. In fact it was in his church that I had attended AA meetings. Why not approach him? He would be my spiritual adviser. This was a big thought. I was excited. I was about to take a big step.

I got up from my chair and started out the door. I was actually in motion when another thought stopped me. "We found it very desirable to take this spiritual Step with an understanding person, such as our wife ..."

Our wife. My wife is not an alcoholic. We had been married only a few months when I came into AA. She had stuck by me during the horrible, wretched, insane days of my drinking; she had stuck to me faithfully and wondrously all during my AA life. She herself, being sensitive and highly intelligent, had staunchly embraced the AA way of life. Yet when I had read the passage in the book I had flipped her out of my mind. I was angry with her, of course. She had upset me. I would get even with her by by-passing her for a minister whom I barely knew. I didn't reason it out that way. I was too resentful for reasoning.

But now it flashed into my consciousness, that phrase "such as our wife." It jolted me to a standstill. I turned around, marched back into the house and went to my wife. I told her what had happened. I showed her the book. We went over the passage and sat down and discussed ourselves. And then we said a prayer, asking our Higher Power for help. We felt better. We decided then and there that, come hell or high water, we would meet every day and ask our Higher Power for help. We would meet under the scriptural aegis, "whenever two or more of you are gathered in my name ...."

At first our thought was to change the attitude of others toward us. How do you do that? By praying for them. So we prayed for them. Then we began widening the circle of people for whom we prayed. We prayed for everybody. We knew that by making our prayer all inclusive we included ourselves. In a roundabout way we were thus getting closer to the spirit of the Eleventh Step, seeking a conscious contact with our Higher Power.

Tensions, which had been running high in the household, eased off. The odd thing was that our prayers seemed to be affecting others as well as ourselves. There was a decided atmospheric improvement, but months went by without noticeable changes. Then things began to happen—disagreeable things, however, flattening things—one frustration after another—rebuffs so violent and arbitrary that they could not be taken as accidental. A project on which I was working collapsed on the verge of triumphant success; an article on which I had labored was accepted by the editor and turned down by the publisher—our financial condition was worsening. Along in January we made a desperate decision: We would go to the Bahamas and find an inexpensive place to live for the rest of our lives. We had an income, so why not? The only trouble was that the Bahamas proved as costly if not more so than the big city. Searching ourselves ruthlessly we had to conclude we were not very honest, not very sane. We had chosen an expensive resort area in which to economize; we mistook sunshine and beautiful beaches as a cure for spiritual ulcers. As far as worry was concerned we were worse off than before.

We met a missionary priest on one of these islands. I recounted to him our series of rebuffs and said, wryly, that it looked to me as if someone from Mars were trying to signal us.

"Do you really believe that?" said the priest, knowing that my observation was veiled and that by the visitor from Mars I really meant God. I said, "Yes, I do," and he said, "Then you will get your answer. You will be surprised."

This remark kept us in balance through many a dark day. It helped to reinforce our initial decision to make our session a daily practice. Out of the 365 days we missed only one. That was due to a virus at Christmas time. We set aside a period after breakfast, while the day was still fresh with promise. Sometimes this was difficult.

We traveled a lot. At one point we were cruising on a forty–foot yawl in Bahamian waters. The skipper and his wife were the other passengers. The only privacy we had was in our bunks, up forward. We had to snatch a few minutes after waking, leaning across from bunk to bunk, and whispering the "Alcoholics Anonymous is a fellowship of men and women ... etc." and a prayer, since anything louder than a whisper could be heard in the calm of our morning anchorage.

At another time, while traveling by bus through the South, we left our hotel one morning in such a rush to catch the bus that we didn't have time for a session and saw no opportunity of having one until nightfall. So at the depot we stood in a huddle before a baggage locker, the door of which was open, and while pretending to be preoccupied with our luggage we managed to engage in a whispered meeting. Well, the missionary was right. It was quite a surprise to find ourselves, four months later, on another island, 5,000 miles away; an island whose name we didn't even know at that time. How we got there is another story, though my wife and I are firmly convinced that those daily sessions are responsible. We had to be uprooted, upturned. I am convinced, too, that only those successions of reversals could have blasted us out of our old habits, our fearsome clinging to what we possessed, even though we knew these possessions were slipping from us.

It happened so simply that we hardly realized it at the time. One day in the Caribbean I was looking through the AA World Directory when I chanced on the name of a loner on an island in the Pacific. He answered fully and completely, and to such satisfaction that we packed up and joined him. And here we found a new life. Economically and in every other way it is beyond our fondest imaginings. Better still, we arrived on the scene as our loner friend was miraculously recovering from near-death-by-accident. We feel we have been helpful to him, and that the opportunity was God-given to us. We are learning to deal with money matters; we are learning, as it is noted in the *Twelve Steps and Twelve Traditions,* to make money our servant rather than our master. We do not expect to be here forever, any more than we expect to be any place forever.

But we are not trying to tell God how to manage us; we are trusting him to tell us. We feel pretty sure that if he could get us onto a Pacific isle he can get us off it if need be.

Anonymous

Meetings in the Bank

June 2009

In July 2008, I went into the hospital for hip replacement surgery. At the time, I had been sober over 12 years, so I knew to do all the things I was supposed to do, such as share my addiction history with my surgeon and my fears and anxieties with my home group. I talked at length with other people who had gone through similar procedures.

But as someone I admire once said, "We always worry about the wrong things." My worries about pain medication never materialized. Twenty-four hours after surgery, I was off epidural pain meds and onto oral medication. I weaned off the pills steadily and diligently.

You know the old expression about "having meetings in the bank"? I now know what that means. It means having meetings in the bank just in case things turn up to disturb your regular routine, and you can't get to your normal group for a couple of days. It does not apply to the upheaval of surgery. When you're in the hospital for five days, that bank is not accessible. You need visitors, you need the phone.

And here's why. My disease was clever enough to wait for all the program people and doctors and nurse to leave, to make sure I was alone, and to sit on the edge of my hospital bed in the middle of the night—when I had nowhere to go—and tell me the surgery was a mistake and I would never leave alive.

I prayed and breathed and cried and shook my hands to try and brush it away. The only thing that could chase my disease was the sun rising on a new morning. Just like when I was counting days 12-plus years ago, and I would wake up and think, Hey, I made it. Grateful, of course, but willful. As I look back now and then, I wish one of those 2 A.M.s I had picked up the phone and called another alcoholic or intergroup. Maybe you will.

After almost four years of limping through life, I walk the Road of Happy Destiny free, light, and out of pain. The walk of a sober man, who recovered from surgery quickly in the middle of the long, slow recovery others have always wished upon him.

Bill S.
New York, New York

SECTION 6

Steps to Serenity

It's particularly satisfying to receive compelling descriptions of the hard-to-describe from our talented members who write in the Grapevine. "My resentments and terror have given way to peace, my fears are being replaced by faith, and my despair is changing to joy," says the author of "Gratitude Was Key." Or, "I applied the ointment of the Twelve Steps to try to bring my emotions to maturity. I became a student, not a teacher. A patient, not a doctor," writes another.

"I work the Steps when I start to hurt," says P.W. from Ohio, formerly a cop-fighting, child-abusing inmate who survived not only divorce but also being disowned by a family who didn't like her sober. Sobriety showed up in her corner.

The author of "What of the Last Half?" describes trying to regain a position of respect, usefulness, security, and happiness in a world from which he had expelled himself. Sometimes emotional sobriety is closely related to common sense, which is most uncommon among active alcoholics, and which can be found in abundance in the Twelve Steps. Another member adds that the Steps offer one of the greatest gifts of all: the ability to stop putting ourselves down, solving the problem of our denying our self-worth.

Then there's this, written by a legally blind member who's just found out that eventually she will live in total blindness: "I've lost my sight, but I've learned to see more. My life is full because my spirit is filled with God. When I feel bad, it's because I allow myself to do so. God waits for me to let him in and lifts me up. So, for those who still struggle with negative 'tapes' playing in their heads, keep on living the Steps and let your Higher Power fill your spirit. The echoes of those words get lighter and lighter—it works, but we have to live it."

Gratitude Turns the Key

April 2010

When I was sober for a few months, I heard that if I did nothing except Step work each morning for a few minutes, that would be OK. So I did, and it was. Now I know that prayer and meditation are the key to relieving the lifelong fear and dread that had consumed me. And they are the key to removing the rest of my character defects.

Gratitude turns the key. By deciding to promptly thank God for any and every situation he brings into my life, I short-circuit my dangerous faulty thinking. Then I can look past the immediate drama right to its acceptance, and sometimes, if God grants me the grace, to its approval—not just in words, but genuinely. If I look for the good and I look inside myself, I will always find something of value in the external situation.

Today I try to look inside first, because I've made the decision to trust God's word and the Promises in the Big Book—not sometimes, but always. I ask that whatever I find that is not a spiritual value, such as selfishness, resentment, or dishonesty, be removed, and I ask for the right thought or action. In this way, God is removing character defects that get in the way of my usefulness to him.

Then I look for the good in any bad situation, and ask that God use it for his purposes, not mine. Either I get a miracle and the situation clears of itself or I find a pesky defect has returned and I'm more ready than ever to work Steps Six and Seven.

In this way, in spite of myself, I have been led to a happy marriage to a kind, loving man who encourages and supports my program of recovery. My once-strained family relationships are now mostly close and joyous, and I've cultivated rich friendships with like-minded people.

My resentments and terror have given way to peace, my fears are being replaced by faith, and my despair is changing to joy.

The Eleventh Step helped me back to the love and trust I had in my youth. But I'm not returning in innocence. I know that life has its heights and its depths and its cycles. That's simply life.

Now I'm secure in knowing that a Higher Power loves and cares for me, always and in all ways.

And now I have faith that no matter what the situation looks like for the moment, there's always some good in it, and that it or I will change for the better if I clearly choose it.

Marie N.
Puerto Vallarta, Mexico

A Bend in Recovery Road

January 1986

When I came through the doors of AA, I had nothing, literally. My three children had been in foster homes and other places because of my inability to care for them. I don't remember fixing meals or buying clothes, and today I don't know how they raised themselves because I was a bar drinker and never home. I had a husband who was in and out of the hospital, and I visited him only because I wanted his workmen's comp checks so I could have money for gas and drinks. I had sold the house when he was in the hospital, and for a while six people lived in a matchbook, two-bedroom house that I rented. I didn't care; I wasn't there. My favorite bar was a block down the road. I became a violent drunk. I would fight with anybody about anything. I abused my children and my husband. In the end, I was fighting cops. After spending a week in jail and really feeling the humiliation of being searched and watched, even in the shower, I was back at the bar the very day I was let out. I never understood. I didn't want to be there. I had a family, I wanted to be home taking care of them, and I could not stay home. Death seemed too good for me. I felt that life was my punishment; I was destined to live because I was such a bad person.

I had trouble when I first came to AA because I thought I was bad trying to be good, instead of sick trying to get better. My recovery was slow because I wouldn't listen, and through my emotional outbursts I was trying to get people to show how much they cared. Today, I know it was because of low self-esteem that I thought no one could love me. Thank God for the people with the patience.

At the age of twenty-seven, when I arrived in AA, I did not have one friend left, not even an acquaintance. I stayed sober my first year because I wanted the approval of the few friends I had made. As one catastrophe after another hit my life in a period of eight months, my sobriety changed drastically and my life improved.

First, my husband filed for divorce and custody of the children. He hated me drunk, but it wasn't anything like he hated me sober. I had to go to court, and the very thing that saved my life was being used against me to take the children I had grown to love. My sponsor died a few months later. I hadn't known she was ill, and no one wanted to tell me because they knew how dependent I was on her. So, when she died I was unprepared, and full of loss. My parents disowned me a couple of months later because I just couldn't do what they wanted me to. They didn't want their daughter going to "those meetings." Never mind that I hadn't been in a fight, jail, or any trouble since coming into the Fellowship. They wanted me to move home and live happily ever after with them; as long as they ran my life, we would all be fine. A month after that, the man I had started seeing (and had transferred most of my dependency onto) said he had enough and wanted to date other women. I fixed that by trying to beat the hell out of him. And I was still sober. I hit an emotional bottom, and in sheer pain and desperation I surrendered to God as I understood him. Period. My dependent self had finally found someone to love and take care of me, and he wouldn't die or leave me alone. For the first time in my life, I felt secure.

Where am I now? I use the Third Step prayer every morning. I work the Steps when I start to hurt. I love to tell people what AA has brought to me, on the inside and on the outside: friends—true, close friends.

My children are with me and we are getting better together. My parents still aren't speaking to me, but I believe in God's time, in his way, it will be okay. The man I loved and cared about in the only way I knew has asked me to marry him. I love and care about him in a totally different way today. I can depend on him, but am not dependent on him. I have recently moved out of a low-income housing development to a real trailer (it was my sponsor's; don't tell me God doesn't love me). The coffeepot is always on for other people like me who are walking the road to recovery.

P. W.
Ashtabula, Ohio

What of the Last Half?

October 1949

Frank stormed out of his client's office snarling, "That stupid, stubborn so-and-so ..." and slammed the door viciously behind him. The jarring impact of the banging door instantly acted as a red signal. Hastily he reopened the door and said to the little man, scowling and scrambling papers on his desk, "Pardon me for slamming the door."

The man glared vacantly, Frank nodded and passed quietly out into the hall and on his way. The dispute that had been raging for three hours had not been settled. An important business relationship teetered in the balance. But Frank got back to his office without a drink.

Nor did he write the scathing letter he had intended to write when he slammed his client's door. He waited until the following day when his sense of humor had returned, and with it some semblance of serenity, patience and tolerance, honesty and self-valuation, positive thinking and a bit of humility. When he finished dictating the rather lengthy letter, he leaned back in his chair and moved his lips inaudibly, "Thy will be done."

It's not important really whether or not Frank retained that account. But it is important to note that he had accepted the fact that he is an alcoholic, and as such it is necessary to safeguard his precious sobriety by sincerely attempting to "practice these principles" in all his daily affairs.

Evidence of this character change might be observed in Frank's attitude toward his landlord who had refused to redecorate, or in his whistle as the elevator man kept him waiting on the 17th floor, in his comments regarding the editor of his favorite newspaper with whose policies he didn't agree, or in his reaction toward his wife who suggested that he forego his fishing trip this weekend and take the family to visit the inlaws.

Frank's fresh attitude in relation to seemingly inconsequential matters or tremendously serious affairs had on occasions been misinterpreted. "This 'Easy Does It' stuff and 'First Things First' philosophy is all right," growled Frank's boss one day, "but don't you think he's carrying it too far?"

Frank didn't believe so, because he was working a desperately serious program—a program of recovery. He was trying to regain a position of respect, usefulness, security, and happiness in a world from which he had expelled himself. And if his program indicated a moment or two of meditation during a heated conference, or even for a missed bus, he realized that his new attitude toward his fellow man would be reflected in continued sobriety.

But sobriety for Frank is now not enough. He has learned that there is a greater and vastly more important victory to be won, that of living with his fellow man unselfishly, with tolerance and understanding. He knows that discretion in the use of tolerance is necessary if he is to continue practicing these principles in all his affairs. For there are times when he has to make a decision between good and bad, and he has discovered that there was just as much harm in being tolerant of wrong thinking and acting as there was in being intolerant of right action.

"That is what is known as common sense," said Frank, "and is one of the essentials in practicing all of the Twelve Steps."

What are these "principles" with which Frank is so concerned in practicing? This is his manner of itemizing them: After acknowledging one's sickness as alcoholism and deciding to do something about it, a study of moral defects of character is made; these are admitted to oneself, God, and another human being; then the realization is made that great physical, mental, and spiritual injury has been inflicted upon oneself and others; but willingness to make amends is expressed and sanity, happiness, and constructive living are achieved through an improved conscious contact with God.

Then these experiences are shared with others, and one practices these principles in all his affairs. Frank believes this can be identified as a spiritual experience, and he is living the AA program up to the hilt.

To keep these principles in action every day, in every contact he makes, would rate Frank a seat somewhere between Gabriel and God. But the fact that he continues to reach for this exalted altitude proves he's making progress in his new way of life. Because in his changed attitude toward his fellow man, Frank has enlarged his spiritual concepts to include a sincere willingness to "practice these principles in all his affairs."

R.G.M.
New York, New York

Confessions of a Reluctant Newcomer

March 2003 (Excerpt)

After treatment, I became, for the second time, a newcomer to AA. A little more desperate than I had been during my first "visit," I made a little more effort to, as Eddie B. said, join the group. In time, I made the shocking discovery that I had little to offer anyone in AA. I knew a lot about books, philosophy, and politics, but nothing about staying or living sober. And until I acquired a degree of humility and became a student, not a teacher; a patient, not a doctor, I would remain ignorant. Intellectually astute (though not as astute as I thought), I was, and sometimes still am, an emotional basket case. I discovered that I was emotionally disturbed, my personality discolored by my reactions to the things that happened to me. I applied the ointment of the Twelve Steps to try to bring my emotions to maturity (and have made progress, but little perfection). No longer a newcomer, I now know through experience that with the help of the Fellowship, the Twelve Steps, and a Higher Power ... I do not have to be a newcomer again.

Wayne B.
Montpelier, Vermont

Step Three: From Sight to Insight

March 2007

Step Three continues to be the most important Step for me. Although the other Steps are important, accepting God and giving up my will makes my life more manageable. I've experienced some bumps along the way, but I have many joys for which I am grateful. If my life were all joy, I'd probably be bored. Challenging times have helped me grow the most. As bad as things may sometimes get, I feel peace inside because I have a history and relationship with my Higher Power, God.

One major challenge has been the loss of my sight. After seventeen surgeries, I've been declared legally blind in my left eye, with half my field of vision. In my right eye I have no vision at all. I never asked, "God, why me?" Instead, I prayed, "God, please be with me and help me get through this." I also asked him not to take all of my sight. It's been quite a journey.

We come to AA to get sober, but within AA we find tools to help us live life. We find a Fellowship that gives love and support. It's up to us what we do with the tools.

Although I've had many growing pains, I've also had far more joy than I ever imagined possible. God loves me and supports me. When I'm weak, he either carries me or, as I've said many times, walks directly behind me, kicking me in the butt to keep me moving. Sometimes I feel like a toddler learning to walk. I take a few steps and fall on my backside. Sometimes I have to sit there for a while. But then I get up and walk again. My legs feel wobbly at times, but the more I do it, the stronger I feel.

Living sober is different from living dry. I choose to turn my will and life over to the care of God today, but God won't hand things to me if I stay in bed and cover my head. I still need to do the legwork. Now, I do things that I never would have dreamed of doing and I see things I've never seen before. I've lost my sight, but I've learned to see more. My life is full because my spirit is filled with God. When I feel bad, it's because I allow myself to do so. God waits for me to let him in and lifts me up. So, for those who still struggle with negative "tapes" playing in their heads, keep on living the Steps and let your Higher Power fill your spirit. The echoes of those words get lighter and lighter—it works, but we have to live it.

I've recently been diagnosed with a disease that will take away my central vision. Since I have no peripheral vision, the impending loss of my central vision is devastating news. It's frightening, but I know I'll be okay. I hate having to accept it, but if I don't, I'm just making my life more difficult. I've cried and will probably do so again.

I'm planning a "scream date" with some AA friends who also have some medical and physical challenges going on. Some people might think we are crazy, but AA taught me to feel my feelings, release them, and then let them go. So, we're going to scream!

Other people ask, "How do you let go and let God? Does it mean throwing caution to the wind?" No, I tell them, but I've learned that worrying about a situation won't change it. I do all that I can and then give the rest to God. And the way I do that is to practice, practice, practice.

For me, the AA program is positive repetition. Each time I live the Steps and allow my Higher Power to help, life is less of a struggle.

Before I came to AA, I knew the meaning of dread. Today, I look at life through the eyes of a child. A leaf, a rock, a handful of dirt, a flower, or a bird is new and exciting. I can't see birds anymore, but I can enjoy their sounds. I can't see the stars, but I know they are there. I can't see snowflakes, but I can feel them on my face.

Although I don't know what tomorrow will bring, I know that there will be AA and I know that there will be God. I may not have a choice in whether I lose my sight or not, but I can choose how to handle it.

Cheryl Lynn F.
Wallkill, New York

Self-Acceptance

June 1975

Almost everyone I know has, in time, experienced some change in his or her thinking on the Steps. Nothing at all unusual about that. It's part of getting better. But little did I realize how very radical a change was in store for me, particularly with respect to the Fourth through Seventh "inventory" Steps.

Why take a personal inventory? Yesterday, I'd have had to grope for an answer, at least one that I found satisfactory. My uncertainty would have been understandable, since yesterday's point of view was essentially negative. It went something like this:

Step Four—"Stop kidding yourself, Buster. It's time you came to grips with reality. You're really not quite as good a person as you'd have yourself believe. So stop trying to convince yourself you are. Take an honest look at all that's basically wrong in your makeup. While you're at it, consider your assets, too—if you can find any."

Step Five—"I'm impatient, intolerant, and so on. To sum it up, there's a lot that's wrong with me. And the worst of it is, I don't want to believe it."

Step Six—"I've done Four and Five as best I can, so I am entirely ready to have all these defects of character removed. At least, I think I'm ready."

Step Seven—"I'm really not sure why, but I'm awfully uncomfortable. I can't seem to do anything about it. Please, God, take it away."

At the time, I heard it said that the alcoholic doesn't put any value on himself, and I thought: Not so. I couldn't see that the truth of this statement was being demonstrated in my own self-rejection. My thinking had to change before I'd be able to do so. And that's just what happened in another encounter with Steps Four, Five, Six, and Seven. The end result was an entirely different point of view, one that's far more acceptable to me. Here's how I look at these Steps today:

Step Four—"It's time you stopped putting yourself down. Basically, you're a good person. So stop trying to convince yourself otherwise. Take an honest look at the garbage you've been holding on to and recognize it for what it is—garbage, not you. While you're at it, consider all that's right in your makeup, and be grateful for it."

Step Five—"I've been denying my own worth. This is the exact nature of my wrongs."

Step Six—"I'm as ready as I can be today to value myself as a human being. But I can't overcome my negative thinking without God's help."

Step Seven—"Dear God, please help me to see me, to accept and be me."

From negative to positive thinking, but it didn't happen overnight. Getting there took time, effort, and some pain. It was well worth it, though. I finally had my answer to the question "Why take an inventory?" To be able to accept myself once and for all, that's why! As a result, I've little room for the old habit of self-rejection in my life today.

Of course, your own interpretation may be a far cry from either of these. That's fine. It is, after all, an individual program. The name of the game is using what helps us stay sober today. And while we readily share our views, perhaps one of the nicest things about the AA program is that we don't always have to agree with each other.

Dick C.
Brooklyn, New York

SECTION 7

Finding Our Inner Adult

The undesirable alcoholic qualities described in the "Twelve and Twelve" might sound familiar to anyone who's been to a nursery school. That famous list may not be welcome news when we're first getting sober, but to those who count on their emotional sobriety to build them a new life, it serves as a warning as we check our attitudes regularly for signs of an inner child tantrum. And we find that evidence much too often.

In another Grapevine book, *Voices of Long-Term Sobriety,* a member writes, "It was there my real adult life began." He was talking about an alcoholic ward in a hospital, where he spent six days at the age of 34 and where one of the visitors to his bedside was Dr. Bob. Most would consider that kind of hospital stay a downer, but because that is where he began to grow up, he blesses it every day.

Bill W. has written that immaturity is the number one symptom of self-obsession. Only an adult can deal with life on life's terms, which is a hallmark of emotional sobriety. It's been also pointed out that the Traditions were written with mature members in mind.

In this chapter is a story from a member who recognizes that his profanity is a measure of his immaturity, and another from a member who recalls his mantra as a newcomer: "They don't know how sensitive I am." And then, with the help of a no-nonsense sponsor, he gets it. "I was not a tragic, noble figure, but ... a self-obsessed middle-aged man who had never grown up."

There are ancillary rewards for such realizations, as well. Old-timers enjoy reminding resistant newcomers of a bonus: Only grownups can win "the cash and prizes."

A Measure of Growth

December 1975

My use of profanity tells on me. During my drinking days, the further I sank into drunkenness, the nastier became my language. I've witnessed the same phenomenon in others. It seems to me that the more blunt my adjectives became, the more I was consumed with hate and fear.

It's a matter of degree, I'm sure. A good healthy "God damn it" never hurt anyone under some moment of emotional stress. And I may greet an old friend, especially from my waterfront days, with, "You old s.o.b., how the hell are you?" These terms in their proper context don't seem to bother me. But the blunt four-letter expletives do. D. H. Lawrence opened a Pandora's box with *Lady Chatterley's Lover.* According to one biography about him, when he spent some time aboard ship with a moviemaking crowd, he was shocked at their carrying on and, I presume, at their language.

All the so-called freedom of expression we're said to be enjoying seems but a license to let it all hang out. I'm sure that living should strike some sort of balance, a golden mean. I realize that I have to know about the extremes, because there might come a time to use extreme measures. But to use extreme language on everyday occasions, for me, would show that I still had hate and carping criticism as part of my personality, that I hadn't come very far in our program. I might be dry, but I would have a long way to go to healthy sobriety, to maturity.

If I had to use the blunt four-letter words, it would suggest that I still had a lot of growing up to do, that I might be the college youngster still trying to shake up the old folks. I sometimes wonder where the youngsters think we were in our early years—in a vacuum? The main difference, I suppose, was that during my rebellious period of life, I happened to be in the Navy, and that was before Admiral "Z," when a bread-and-water diet and confinement in the brig were the therapy administered to rebels.

Yes, I had a very nasty mouth in those days, and vestiges remained during my first marriage. It took liberal doses of alcohol to loosen restraints during parties, so that my shadowy Mr. Hyde could come staggering out and hold forth on any subject at hand. On politics, art, or good conduct, the complete, instant authority became manifest with sloshing drink in hand, brooking no argument. It's a wonder we were invited back as often as we were. Perhaps I was on the entertainment calendar. I should have learned to juggle plates or tap-dance instead; either would have caused less wear and tear on the old liver and gray matter.

Therefore, you salty dogs who wish to punctuate with profanity, have at it. But don't look now, because your immaturity might be showing, as well as a limited vocabulary.

Sam M.
Safford, Arizona

How It Feels to Join AA Long Before You Have To

November 1944

It was a lovely spring morning last June, warm and full of promise—a day that fills you with love of life and a desire to live it fully, to accomplish all the things you have dreamed, to work, to love your fellow man. It was the first day of my vacation after a busy year—a vacation eagerly planned for and set aside to do a piece of creative work that was a joy to me. The night before there had been a late party to celebrate the finish of the old and the bright beginning of the new. I was shaky that morning, having celebrated thoroughly, so before I started to shop for my new equipment I decided to have a martini or two before lunch. I awoke at twilight with a bewildered sense of loss. The lovely day was gone. A shiver of terror went through me and then the slow, steady creep of smothering panic. Something terrible was the matter with me but WHAT? This wasn't the first time this had happened in spite of my best intentions and plans. It had happened with increasing frequency whenever I was released from responsibility. A cold, damp sweat folded around me like a blanket and I was filled with violent nausea. Later I phoned the liquor store. I had to have a drink so I could think this through clearly.

At the end of a week with days beginning and ending in the same way I was reduced to despair and gibbering panic. I couldn't go out in the street, let alone ride in a bus. I was afraid to get in an elevator. I couldn't sit in a movie for fear of screaming out loud. Safe in the apartment the walls started moving in on me. The long vacation yawned ahead like a dark valley of horror. In my despair I doubted if I'd find myself alive at the end of it, let alone well and ready for work. There was no reality but the fight between me and my panic, and the only weapon I knew to fight it with was a drink. I had had psychoanalysis and supposedly should not be suffering this recurrence of panic, but it was worse than in its original form. There was no further help to be sought from that angle. Slowly a thought had begun to focus in my terrified mind. Could the panic have any relationship to my drinking?

I didn't believe it for a moment, but in my despair I couldn't afford to ignore the possibility. If that were all, then everything was simple. I'd just stop drinking and things would straighten out.

I hated to stop drinking, of course, because I actually enjoyed everything about it: the taste, the smell, and the effect that gave me a sense of well-being, gaiety, and courage, for I suffered from an awful shyness and tension with people. Also, liquor had been a daily part of my life for years; helping me through difficulties, being a reward for work well done and a solace when I was depressed. In fact, as I thought about it, liquor was a pretty constant companion in good health and ill, for better or for worse. It went on weekends with me and came home with me. It was waiting for me after work and spent many evenings with me when I should have been following some of my other interests. It frequently went to bed with me and was there in the morning whenever I needed it in the last couple of years. It had lunch with me when it could. It monopolized my vacations because I was carefree. I took it with me where I knew I wouldn't find it. Several times I decided that a temporary vacation would do me good, but I never stayed away more than several days.

Generally, it had been a good companion, reliable and restrained for years, especially when I had work to do. It indulged itself on weekends and at parties and plagued me with hang-overs—some pretty bad ones in the last two years, but it had never interfered with a job or made me sick for more than a holiday or Sunday. It hadn't separated me from my friends or landed me in a hospital. My doctor had never discussed it with me, having no reason to, and my analyst had told me that it was not the factor in my disturbance, though it might be wise not to drink so regularly. But now I made up my mind to stop drinking entirely for the rest of my vacation. To my horror I found I couldn't. The decision to do so seemed to enhance terrifically the desire to drink and all I accomplished was to make of myself a battle ground—one part of me fighting to drink and the other part fighting not to drink. The battle lasted one day and that night I got plastered. The victor rode the field for a week in varying degrees of being slightly tight to being drunk. I never passed out, but I kept trying through the fog to figure out what in hell had broken loose. One side of me was making a souse out of me with all the symptoms, while the other was reeling around helplessly.

Then I remembered reading about AA and hearing that a friend of mine had joined. I phoned and went to see her—not, of course, telling her the whole story, but inquiring about symptoms. She advised attending a meeting, where I behaved like the patient outside the dentist's office who decides he doesn't have a toothache after all. I fought every identification of myself with alcoholism. I had stopped drinking with no effort after the second meeting and for two weeks I attended every meeting with the sole purpose, I recognize now, of proving to myself that I wasn't an alcoholic. But in that time I read the book several times and began to follow the program. I talked with other members, but nowhere could I get what I wanted—a flat, factual statement that I was or was not an alcoholic, in their opinion. It seemed that I had to decide for myself with the wealth of knowledge and experience spread before me at meetings, talks, and in the literature. Then, suddenly, I had to go away for two weeks and I began to drink again with the friends I was visiting. But something had happened to me. Sometimes I think you get this program through the pores by just going to meetings, being with members, and keeping your mind and heart as open as you can. Once you get inside, as my father used to say to us kids: "The Lord has you by the hand!" Something bigger than myself certainly had me by the hand. I stopped drinking with my friends and began the work I had wanted to do—placing my whole problem in the care of the Power greater than myself of which I had heard so much. My mind cleared, an unknown sense of peace quietly took hold of me, and my work went well. I humbly followed the 24 hour plan and asked no questions of myself or IT as to what path I was being lead along or what it signified.

That was two months ago. I returned to AA, so glad to be back and with no inner resistance. Since then I have attended all the meetings that my work permits, have started some Twelfth Step work, and have grown to know many people and to depend upon their help and wisdom when I am frightened, troubled, or depressed. The panic has gone and I have no desire to drink now, though I don't avoid parties and situations where there is drinking. There is a new, fresh interest in my job, an unexpected reserve of material and ideas for it, and an unexpected energy of a different quality—deep, easy, and relaxed. Most important of all is a consciousness of a growing experience with a Power outside myself, which I depend upon and trust and which takes over for me things that are too much for me—more things than my drinking. All this fills me with awe and a profound gratitude to AA for this new and happy life I am living.

Beatrice

Grow Up!

June 1999

My sponsor, Bill, and I were driving south on California's old Interstate 5 in late February of 1970. The bright moonlight reflected on the surface of the mighty Pacific Ocean, and the two-lane highway was practically empty. We were returning from the legendary Laguna Beach Men's Stag meeting, where Bill and I drove faithfully each Monday night. What a gathering of old-timers that meeting was. Thirty or so men, all with twenty years sobriety or more. These were the original pioneers of AA in Southern California, and they were tough men with AA dedication.

It was not the type of meeting that a pompous, over-educated, negative newcomer like myself would choose to attend. It terrified me each week, but I showed up because I was even more terrified of my sponsor. Many evenings these old-timers would lie in the weeds waiting for me (or one of the other newcomers) to whine and snivel about some real—or fancied—difficulty in our lives. Then, like blood-starved sharks, they would rip us apart. With great glee, they would point out to us our selfishness and shallowness. I was more often than not the object of their attack, because I was the primary sniveler and whiner. That night, they had drawn and quartered me.

In the darkness of the car I blurted out, "They don't know how sensitive I am." My sponsor didn't answer, he looked straight ahead. There was, however, a tiny muscle jumping just above his right eye. As the years rolled by, I came to know and recognize this twitch as a signal to me to shut up and smile, but being new and self-obsessed, I decided he hadn't heard and so I repeated, "They just don't know how sensitive I am."

Bill was a great shouter. He could shatter eyeglasses with sheer decibels. But this time, he turned toward me, there in that darkened car, and pushed his sentences through his clenched teeth. He said, "Let's get this straight. You are not sensitive. You are an immature SOB."

My Al-Anon wife calls this kind of episode a Kodak moment—those unforgettable incandescent instances we hold forever clearly in our mind's eye; those golden moments that have snatched life back from the gates of insanity and death for us survivors. I can visualize the car, Bill's eyes, the road, the shining Pacific. Now, many sober years later, I remember that moment, and that night. Because I didn't want a lonely, drunken death, I accepted Bill's premise: I was not a star-crossed, tragic, noble figure, but instead, a self-obsessed middle-aged man who had never grown up.

The dictionary's first definition of immaturity is "not fully grown or developed," and that is the story of my life! For whatever reasons—psychological, social, or spiritual—I never reached a level of maturity that would allow me to live in the world on the world's terms. I was always baffled by the problems of life that other people seemed to solve with impunity. After I discovered the magical properties of booze, I had no need to seek solutions. I had a ready-made solution in a shot glass. And because I was incapable of accepting the "slings and arrows of outrageous fortune," I returned to that shot glass again and again. I had seen myself as tragic rather than pitiful. I had imagined myself abused rather than self-destructive. I had been a victim, not a volunteer.

I didn't sleep that night. At dawn I got up and took a cup of coffee out to the back stairs. As the sun began to push the darkness back, I whispered a muddled prayer to the power of the universe. I asked the power to please help me grow up.

A few nights later, I heard a man speak on the Twelve Steps of AA. Sometime during the course of that night, it came to me that these Steps were provided by a loving Higher Power to help people like me mature.

Now, approaching my twenty-ninth sober year, I remember all those newcomers that I have Twelfth-Stepped, all of those men I have sponsored, all the Fifth Steps I have heard, and I know without a shadow of a doubt that Bill W. was absolutely correct when he stated that self-obsession is the number one defect of character in alcoholics, and

I further believe that immaturity is the number one symptom of self-obsessed people.

Bill W. also wrote that if AA fails it will not be because of pressures or problems from outside but rather as a result of failures from within. As my years in the Fellowship have gone by, I have come to one conclusion: if AA fails it will be because too many of us remain immature. The Traditions of AA were written with mature members in mind. They depend upon people who are willing to sacrifice their own comfort and their own selfish ambitions for the good of the group and the good of the newcomer. Immature people have a great deal of trouble suppressing their own selfish impulses for the good of the whole.

We see evidence of this immaturity everywhere. We see it in service positions unfilled. We see it in the small number of groups willing to support AA financially. We see it in the rudeness at meetings. We see it in the sophomoric chanting and counting during AA readings. We see it especially in the increasingly smaller numbers of members available for Twelfth-Step work, and we see it when old-timers refuse to sponsor new people.

My prayer today is that I (and the men I sponsor) continue to grow and mature. I pray that I remember each day that my very life depends on that growth and that the future of AA depends upon my mature actions. I ask the Higher Power for the ability and willingness to accept the First Tradition as a guide to my life.

Cliff R.
Oceanside, California

When I Was 15

September 2010

"I'm pregnant." I still ponder the pre-drawn sudden wakefulness that always followed my binges of drinking and blackout craziness. Was its cause a physiological response to the overindulgence of alcohol or was it an emotional and spiritual response to the unseemly acts that took place during my drinking binges?

Whatever the answer, this is the statement that jolted me awake one August morning in 1973 when I was 15 years old. We had moved to Florida from upstate New York five short days prior. I was very distraught about the move from its inception, being forced to leave all that I loved—a grandma, a boyfriend, a girlfriend, the only school I'd ever known, and a hometown full of my growing up—for what my parents thought was paradise.

The day before, my parents and I had set out to have a day at the beach. We ended up in Cocoa Beach, about a two-hour drive north from where we lived. I remember that there was ocean and sun and sand, and all the along the top portion of the beach, there were bars.

I had begun drinking in New York when I was 14, after being rejected from the cheerleading squad in my freshman year of high school. I had suspected all along that I was not good enough, not only for the cheerleading squad, but for life in general, and this event confirmed it. When I began drinking behind the school during the same basketball games that I had hoped to cheer for, I found the magic that alcohol held for me: release from the "not good enoughs." From that point on, alcohol was my Higher Power.

On the beach, I found myself alone after my parents went off to find their own good time. No cell phones existed to keep in touch and I was left to freely explore. I know today that only my Higher Power kept me alive that day. Over the years since this happened, vague and desperate memories have surfaced of the places alcohol took me that day: to a bar with strange men; into the ocean, drunk and swimming with someone I did not know; searching for my bathing suit top in the ocean waves; in a van having sex; and being involved in a car accident on the way home.

I'm pregnant, I thought the next morning. I knew it from deep within my soul. And so it was.

I was in a new state with not one friend in whom to confide. It was one year after the Supreme Court case of Roe vs. Wade had legalized abortion, but long before it was a widely accepted practice, especially in the deep south. In late September 1973, after an agonizing month of isolation with my secret, I told my parents, and terminated my pregnancy.

Those of you who are familiar with the darkness of alcoholism will understand that the serious nature of this event might have looked like one of those "jumping-off points" that the Big Book speaks of, whereby we are faced with the seriousness of our alcoholism and its consequences and make a decision to change. In fact, this was only the beginning of my journey to hell and back. For 15 more years, I drank and damaged myself and others as only an untreated alcoholic can. However, by the grace of God, I married and conceived three children, all planned and deeply loved.

Through it all, I carried with me the shame, sadness, and pain from that day at Cocoa Beach.

One morning in 1989 when I was 30, after a drinking binge, I was jolted awake in much the same way as I had been on that August morning in 1973. This time, though, it was my Higher Power whom I listened to, and as I looked into the blue eyes of my 9-year-old daughter he gave me the words that I heard myself speak: "Mommy drinks too much and she needs to get help in AA."

"OK," she replied and smiled up at me with the assurance that only a 9-year-old can have when placed up against such a challenge.

I called the AA hotline and within half an hour, word spread along the AA airwaves in our little town and a woman called me, took me to my first meeting that evening, and became my sponsor. From the instant I made the call, I felt a great relief and a great power, and I felt like all would be well. I am sober because I was shown by my sponsor how to trust God, clean house, and help others through the program of Alcoholics Anonymous. I have had the spiritual awakening described in Step Twelve, I carry the message to alcoholics who still suffer, and practice the AA principles in all of my affairs—to the best of my ability, one day at a time. If I don't, I return to my baseline of "restless, irritable, and discontent," and we all know where that ultimately leads: to the first drink. And for me, to drink is to die. In February 2010, I celebrated my 21st year of sobriety.

My story could end here, but there is more. In February 2009, my husband (who has an AA recovery story of his own) and I traveled to Florida for a winter vacation. One night while driving back to our hotel from dinner, a sign caught my eye. It said, "Cocoa Beach—15 miles."

My husband knew of that fateful August day in 1973 and later as we sat on our hotel balcony overlooking the dark night ocean, I asked him if he had seen the sign. He had. "Could we go there?" I asked him, not really knowing why, but sensing an urgency to go.

"Of course," was his reply. "When do you want to go?"

We went the very next day. Our plan was to try to find, using only my very vague memory, the area where I had been so many years before. Even though I had dealt with this misadventure in my Fourth Step many years ago, the proximity to the location stirred the remaining demons inside of me as we drove toward the beach. We parked and walked and sure enough we found the same ocean, sun, sand—and bars. We walked without plan or talk. We went inside one bar and asked about its history. Had it always been there? Under the same name? It wasn't quite right.

We walked back out into the sunshine and there, across the sand, I saw it. Actually, I felt it. We went inside this bar and it was the same one from my desperate memories. My husband stood and waited while I walked across the floor toward the bathroom. I let every ounce of my sobriety flood me and shield me and project me across the floor. As I used the bathroom, I imagined myself as that adolescent girl in her bikini in this bar with strangers, drinking underage and alcoholically, so many years before. My beautiful, loving husband was waiting for me and we went back into the sunshine onto the beach.

As sponsors, my husband and I complete the Twelve Steps with new people using the Big Book of Alcoholics Anonymous in the way that we were shown by our sponsors. After completing the Fifth Step, we burn the Fourth Step list to symbolize the end of the old alcoholic thinking and behaviors. It proves quite emotional for those who are ready to change.

In the hotel the night before, I had written a letter to myself about the tragedy that had occurred on the beach so long ago. I now opened it and read it aloud while my husband held my hand. In it, I asked God to help me forgive that young girl and allow her to be free of the pain and sickness that held her captive. I let go of the lingering resentments toward my parents, whom I felt had deserted me that day, and of the others whom I'd allowed to hurt me. And I thanked God for the life of sobriety that has been so freely given to me today if I but work for it. Together, my husband and I knelt and lit the paper afire. We watched it burn to ashes in silence, we recited the Third Step Prayer and the Seventh Step Prayer.

Then we walked hand in hand across the street to the AA meeting that was about to begin.

A.K.R.
Cooperstown, New York

The Twelve Steps

1. We admitted we were powerless over alcohol—that our lives had become unmanageable.
2. Came to believe that a Power greater than ourselves could restore us to sanity.
3. Made a decision to turn our will and our lives over to the care of God *as we understood Him.*
4. Made a searching and fearless moral inventory of ourselves.
5. Admitted to God, to ourselves, and to another human being the exact nature of our wrongs.
6. Were entirely ready to have God remove all these defects of character.
7. Humbly asked Him to remove our shortcomings.
8. Made a list of all persons we had harmed, and became willing to make amends to them all.
9. Made direct amends to such people wherever possible, except when to do so would injure them or others.
10. Continued to take personal inventory and when we were wrong promptly admitted it.
11. Sought through prayer and meditation to improve our conscious contact with God *as we understood Him,* praying only for knowledge of His will for us and the power to carry that out.
12. Having had a spiritual awakening as the result of these steps, we tried to carry this message to alcoholics, and to practice these principles in all our affairs.

The Twelve Traditions

1. Our common welfare should come first; personal recovery depends upon A.A. unity.
2. For our group purpose there is but one ultimate authority—a loving God as He may express Himself in our group conscience. Our leaders are but trusted servants; they do not govern.
3. The only requirement for A.A. membership is a desire to stop drinking.
4. Each group should be autonomous except in matters affecting other groups or A.A. as a whole.
5. Each group has but one primary purpose—to carry its message to the alcoholic who still suffers.
6. An A.A. group ought never endorse, finance or lend the A.A. name to any related facility or outside enterprise, lest problems of money, property and prestige divert us from our primary purpose.
7. Every A.A. group ought to be fully self-supporting, declining outside contributions.
8. Alcoholics Anonymous should remain forever nonprofessional, but our service centers may employ special workers.
9. A.A., as such, ought never be organized; but we may create service boards or committees directly responsible to those they serve.
10. Alcoholics Anonymous has no opinion on outside issues; hence the A.A. name ought never be drawn into public controversy.
11. Our public relations policy is based on attraction rather than promotion; we need always maintain personal anonymity at the level of press, radio and films.
12. Anonymity is the spiritual foundation of all our traditions, ever reminding us to place principles before personalities.

AA Grapevine

AA Grapevine is AA's international monthly journal, published continuously since its first issue in June 1944. The AA pamphlet on AA Grapevine describes its scope and purpose this way: "As an integral part of Alcoholics Anonymous since 1944, the Grapevine publishes articles that reflect the full diversity of experience and thought found within the A.A. Fellowship, as does La Viña, the bimonthly Spanish-language magazine, first published in 1996. No one viewpoint or philosophy dominates their pages, and in determining content, the editorial staff relies on the principles of the Twelve Traditions."

In addition to magazines, AA Grapevine, Inc. also produces books, eBooks, audiobooks, mobile apps, a weekly podcast, an Instagram account, a YouTube channel and other items. It also offers a Grapevine Complete subscription, which includes the print magazine as well as complete online access, with new stories weekly, AudioGrapevine (the audio version of the magazine), the vast Grapevine Story Archive and current online issues of Grapevine and La Viña. For more information on AA Grapevine, or to subscribe to any of these, please visit the magazine's website at aagrapevine.org or write to:

AA Grapevine, Inc.
475 Riverside Drive
New York, NY 10115

Alcoholics Anonymous

AA's program of recovery is fully set forth in its basic text, *Alcoholics Anonymous* (commonly known as the Big Book), now in its Fourth Edition, as well as in *Twelve Steps and Twelve Traditions, Living Sober,* and other books. Information on AA can also be found on AA's website at www.aa.org, or by writing to:

Alcoholics Anonymous
Box 459
Grand Central Station
New York, NY 10163

For local resources, check your local telephone directory under "Alcoholics Anonymous." Four pamphlets, "This is A.A.," "Is A.A. For You?," "44 Questions," and "A Newcomer Asks" are also available from AA.

Notes: